In
My
Dreams

By
Sherri l Ingram

—

The copyright # for my application is: **1-14154739511**

Copyright © 2024 Sherrilingram

All rights reserved.

Dedication

To Kim and Becky – thank you for your gift of listening to the promptings of the spirit. It is because of you that this journey went from not even a thought, to then being a concept, and finally to a completed product.

To Suzanna, Jennifer, Karen and Jill – thank you for your feedback, your continued encouragement, and your sincere gifts of love and friendship during this process.

To Lori and Lorinda – Thank you for your time and talent in editing and helping me get this book ready.

To my bug – thank you for your encouragement, but also for your amazing gift in turning my vision into a beautiful piece of artwork on the cover.

To Willy – Your belief in my dream meant the world to me. I know you've been behind the scenes in heaven, on the other side of the veil, helping to guide my thoughts, pushing me to continue when I had writers block, and cheering me on when it was finally completed. You are loved and missed every single day, and I cannot wait to celebrate once more when we meet again. Give GG a hug for me!

And to my Jess – I have no words that can adequately express my gratitude for the support, encouragement, patience and love you've always given me. Your belief in my ability to finish this project was instrumental in me not giving up. I loved you first, I love you most, and I'll love you for eternity. XOXO

Reference Information

This book utilizes references from the Old Testament, New Testament, Book of Mormon and the Doctrine and Covenants. All four books are read, studied, and cherished, by members of The Church of Jesus Christ of Latter-Day Saints. Most of the quotes are taken from our Prophet, Apostles and leaders of the Church. Below is a quick explanation, taken from our Church's website, regarding The Book of Mormon and the Doctrine and Covenants.

If you have questions regarding either of these books, or our beliefs, please go to https://www.churchofjesuschrist.org and click on About Us.

The Book of Mormon is a book of inspired scripture that was translated from ancient records by Joseph Smith, Jr. It exists to give us direction in our lives and connect us to Jesus. Where does the name come from? Hundreds of years ago, an ancient prophet named Mormon compiled a record of his people. They faced a lot of the same challenges that we do. And just like us, they found strength when they turned to Jesus Christ.

The Book of Mormon is meant to be read alongside the Bible as another testament of Jesus Christ and His divine mission as the Savior and Redeemer of the world. Together, the Bible and the Book of Mormon provide more understanding of God's great love for all of us and can help us come closer to Him.

The Doctrine and Covenants is a collection of divine revelations and inspired declarations given for the establishment and regulation of the kingdom of God on the earth in the last days. Although most of the sections are directed to members of The Church of Jesus Christ of Latter-day Saints, the messages, warnings, and exhortations are for the benefit of all mankind and contain an invitation to all people everywhere to hear the voice of the Lord Jesus Christ, speaking to them for their temporal well-being and their everlasting salvation.

The book of Doctrine and Covenants is one of the standard works of the Church in company with the Holy Bible, the Book of Mormon, and the Pearl of Great Price. However, the Doctrine and Covenants is unique because it is not a translation of an ancient document, but is of modern origin and was given of God through His chosen prophets for the restoration of His holy work and the establishment of the kingdom of God on the earth in these days. In the revelations, one hears the tender but firm voice of the Lord Jesus Christ, speaking anew in the dispensation of the fulness of times; and the work that is initiated herein is preparatory to His Second Coming, in fulfillment of and in concert with the words of all the holy prophets since the world began.

Table Of Contents

Introduction

From an incredibly young age, I knew there was a God. I, however, was not raised in a religious home. And because of this I never really understood anything related to deity. God was never discussed, and church was never attended. In fact, my home environment was quite the opposite, so understanding who and what God is didn't come without confusion. My innocent, unlearned brain had a belief that God lived in Heaven somewhere above the clouds, and it was where our family went when they died. I also believed that God was in church, so church is where I wanted to be as often as possible.

When I was 6 years of age, we moved to a mobile home park and lived there until after my 10th birthday. I can remember sneaking out to visit the elderly lady who lived behind us. Somehow, I think she knew that I needed God in my life, and she became like an adopted grandmother who would give me cookies and occasionally take me to church with her. She was my first experience with anything related to Christianity.

As the years went by, my desire to know more about God increased, as did the struggles in my home. I continued to go to church with whoever would take me. During the summers, I went to Vacation Bible School and church camp where I learned the stories of Jesus. At some point, I stumbled upon a Baptist church that held youth nights every Wednesday. I will always be grateful for those youth leaders who accepted me as one of their own without question. It was during these youth nights that I learned how to pray and where I memorized the names of the books in the New Testament.

My high school years brought 80's rock music, more anxiety at home, and a violent sexual assault when I was 15 years old. It was also around this time that I bought my very first bible. As my senior year rolled around, I did everything in my power not to be at home. I was still attending different churches, but I began to notice the differences in their beliefs. It was during this time that God blessed me with a classmate who quickly became my best friend. She and I were inseparable that entire year and I came to know her family quite well. This was the kind of family I longed to be a part of; the kind of family that I wanted to have for myself one day. After graduation, she invited me to church and of course, I went. She was a member of The Church of Jesus Christ of Latter-Day Saints. My initial thought was, "Gosh, that's a really long name". After the services ended, I was hooked. When I walked out of that building, I knew I was home, and I never looked back.

My entire childhood was difficult, and at times it felt unbearable. But in retrospect, I can see that I was blessed with tender mercies, and with individuals throughout my adolescence that helped to lead and guide my spiritual footsteps. I saw and lived through situations that no adult should ever experience, let alone a child. I genuinely believe that it is because of these trials, and the inner strength and determination I would need to endure it all, that Heavenly Father blessed me with the sacred gift of dreams and visions. President Thomas S. Monson, an apostle for The Church of Jesus Christ of Latter-Day Saints, once said "When we are on the Lord's errand, we are entitled to the Lord's help. Remember that the Lord will shape the back to bear the burden placed upon it." (General Conference, October 2008, 'To Learn, to Do, to Be.') My back was indeed being shaped to bear my many burdens, but those burdens somehow seemed lighter than they should have been. When I think back to those times in my childhood that often, felt so onerous, I am reminded of when Alma, a prophet from the Book of Mormon, and his people were being persecuted. The Lord said, 'I will also ease the burdens which are put upon your shoulders, that even you cannot feel them upon your backs, even while you are in bondage; and this will I do that ye may stand as witnesses for me hereafter, and that ye may know of a surety that I, the Lord God, do visit my people in their afflictions' (Book of Mormon; Mosiah 24:14).

2

My dreams and visions began when I was a small child, and they have continued through the present day. Even if I never have another, I will be eternally grateful for every dream I have experienced because each one has had significant meaning in my life, and I have received guidance from them many times over. I do, however, hope that Heavenly Father continues to use this gift to lead and guide me on my path going forward. I can only pray to be worthy of such a blessing.

These dreams have brought me comfort during trials, they have given me hope in times of despair, and I have received many reassurances when I had doubts. Some have been answers to prayers, some have been what my future holds, some have been what seem to be completely random experiences (even though I know God does not do random). And recently, my dreams have taken on a new purpose of blessing the lives of others. They have all been very different, but all are confirmations of Heavenly Father's love for me. On occasion, I've even had the opportunity to share these experiences with my sweet husband, and those moments I hold close to my heart. We are constantly reminded that where there is true faith, there will be miracles, visions, dreams, healings, and all the gifts that God blesses His saints with.

It is my hope and prayer that as I share my experiences of learning to know, understand, use, and appreciate the gifts that God has given me, you sincerely ponder and pray about the gifts He has bestowed upon you. Through my studies of the Old and New Testament, the Book of Mormon, and The Doctrine and Covenants, I have learned that even the prophets of old doubted and rejoiced in their talents and gifts, and I hope that you can see your own reflection in their experiences just as I have done. My journey has been frustrating, and beautiful, and heartbreaking, and wonderous, and I would not have it any other way. It is because of life's experiences, and a lot of trial and error and determination, that God has allowed me the opportunity to have a greater appreciation for the gifts that I do have. And I promise that as you put forth the effort to know, understand, use, and appreciate your own gifts, God will open the doors of Heaven wider than you ever thought possible. In moments of doubt, remember that every challenge is an opportunity for growth and a testament to the strength God has instilled in you.

Spiritual gifts are numerous and varied

And come to us as we seek them

And use them appropriately.

We enjoy them because of the power of the

Holy Ghost,

Which is in and around and woven

Through our lives.

Julie B. Beck, "An Outpouring of Blessings"; General Conference, April 2006

Chapter 1

"Never Take Your Eyes Off of Me"

Many years ago, my mom was watching our young daughters while I was working, and my husband was out of town. Through some very unfortunate circumstances, our two-year-old found and ate what she thought was candy. That candy was several different medications that belonged to my grandmother. She was rushed to the hospital where I met up with them shortly thereafter. I was quickly escorted back to my daughter's room as the nurses were attempting to hold her down to get an IV started. She, however, was not being very cooperative and fought against them until she depleted herself of all her strength. I ran over and tried to comfort my little one, as any worried momma would, but all my attempts were futile. She looked at me with alligator tears flowing, turned away and reached for someone on the other side of the bed. Someone that only she could see. I knew in that moment that her tear-filled eyes were drawn to the Savior. That moment was a reminder of a lesson that the Savior taught me when I was not much older than my sweet daughter.

I was very young, around five or six years of age when I had my first spiritual dream. Back then, it would have been impossible for me to understand the significance, but I knew it was something special, and to this day, it remains my most vivid and colorful dream yet.

There were a few of us children walking in a line behind a man dressed in flowing white robes. We walked barefoot through a field of the most vivid, soft green grass, and then up a hill that had a majestic oak tree standing as a sentinel, watching over the beauty of what laid before us. Once we got to the top of the hill, we had a breathtaking view of a crystal teal-green lake with a tropical island in the middle of the water. The sky was a clear, perfect azure blue with a few wispy clouds scattered about. I can remember a soft breeze on my face that also gently blew the robes of the man that was leading us to our destination. I did not know where we were going but I do remember trusting the man, without question. We walked down to the shoreline, and he turned to us and said, "Do not ever take your eyes off of me". His voice was so kind and gentle, and loving, yet strong in his urging for us to obey him. It was like a peace had washed over me as he spoke.

At this point, he turned back around and proceeded to walk across the water. All of us did as we were told, keeping our eyes on the man in white robes, following closely behind him toward the island in the middle of the lake. Once we got to the island, he turned to us again and said, "Not everything is as it seems", and then he was gone.

The island was picturesque with white sandy beaches and palm trees that bent low and curved in all different directions. There were huge seashells and rocks everywhere with beautiful paintings and messages written on them. The only one I recognized was the New Testament scripture of John 3:16, "For God so loved the world, that he gave his only begotten Son, that whosoever believeth in him should not perish, but have everlasting life." The one painted seashell that I can still see in my mind was a Christmas scene of Joseph and Mary watching over baby Jesus as He lay in the manger.

We were all playing in the sand, running in the water, and searching for more shells and rocks when one of the other girls asked if I wanted to explore the island with her. I was so excited to see what other surprises the island held for us that we both went running up an embankment. Just on the other side, we came upon a small, clear blue pond with two dolphins jumping and playing in the water. As I stood there watching them, it seemed as though they were beckoning me to join them. I immediately started running towards the pond but my friend shouted for me to come back. She reminded me of the warning we were given when she yelled, "Remember, not everything is as it seems!" I instantly stopped and turned around only to see a panicked look on her face. I turned back around to watch the dolphins from a distance just as the beautiful pool of water turned into a swamp and the dolphins turn into ugly monsters. And then the dream was over.

I often laugh at the abrupt ending of that dream, but to a five-year-old, it was pretty scary. I did not know it at the time, but eventually came to realize that the man in my dream was the Savior. It took a few years for my little brain to understand the basic primary messages and I do not find it coincidental that the one scripture and painting I remember center so perfectly on Christ. My heart has yearned to remember what was on the other rocks and seashells, but all I can see when I close my eyes are blurry words and pictures that I cannot make out.

It took several more years before I began to comprehend the magnitude of it all as I started to peel back the many layers of doctrine found within the depths of that dream. And once I began to understand the significance of walking on the water with the Savior, I was humbled beyond words. I struggled for many years wondering why I had been blessed with such a sacred moment because I never felt worthy of that gift, but later learned, as my understanding of the gospel matured, that God's love for His children is an infinitely powerful love that can guide us, heal us, and protect us at all times and through many different means, as long as we do as He bid and never take our eyes off of Him. And to this day, I can still hear His beautiful voice in my head as He spoke those simple, yet profound words.

Many of my childhood memories center around family members who struggled with drug and alcohol addictions. I can remember when the Stranger Danger campaign began, followed shortly by McGruff the Crime Dog and then Just Say No to Drugs. It was talked about non-stop in school, and you were guaranteed to see commercials on Saturday mornings in between the cartoons. Everyone preached that drugs were illegal, and bad for you, but they were in my home and just a part of my everyday life. As a small child, how was I supposed to know that my home was anything but normal? It unnerves me to think about the many abhorrent situations that I was exposed to but in hindsight I realize that I was being watched over by the 'man dressed in white robes'. The Savior gave me strict instructions to follow in a way that I could understand at my young age, and those same instructions would apply throughout my life.

When the Savior was visiting the Nephites after His crucifixion, as recorded in the Book of Mormon, the people were able to sit at his feet as He taught them, and soon after, He knelt and said a mighty prayer unto His Father on their behalf. Then, one of the most beautiful moments in the scriptures took place when the Savior of the world:

> …took their little children, one by one, and blessed them, and prayed unto the Father for them. and they saw the heavens open, and they saw angels descending out of heaven as it were in the midst of fire; and they came down and encircled those little ones about, and they were encircled about with fire; and the angels did minister unto them. (Book of Mormon, 3 Nephi 17: 21,24)

The parents of those sweet children watched as the Savior wept over their little ones, prayed unto the Father on their behalf, and then called down the angels to minister unto them, *one by one*. Looking back, I feel as though I was one of those children, being individually blessed by the Savior. I can remember times where it felt as though the angels had descended out of heaven and encircled me with fire in my darkest hours.

Still, to this day, I have to continually remind myself that the Savior's love for His little ones also extends to us as adults. He will administer unto to us, one by one, just as He did those little Nephite children. Let us remember that the Savior is the one who taught us to become as a little child when he said "Except ye be converted, and become as little children, ye shall not enter into the kingdom of heaven. Whosoever therefore shall humble himself as this little child, the same is greatest in the kingdom of heaven" (New Testament, Matt 18:3-4). Just as the Savior ministered to me so long ago, He has maintained His ever-watchful care over the years and will continue to do so throughout my mortality. He has used my spiritual gifts to teach me doctrine, to remind me of my worth, and to extend a hand when I needed His loving touch, with the caveat being my willingness to look to Him in all things.

In the New Testament in Matthew chapter 14, we learn of Jesus walking on the water and Peter, with faith-filled sincerity, asked, "Lord, if it be thou, bid me come unto thee on the water." Jesus simply responded with, "Come". Peter jumped out of the boat and began walking on the water towards Jesus and yet, his faith waivered. "But when he saw the wind boisterous, he was afraid; and beginning to sink, he cried saying Lord, save me" (Matthew 14:28-30). The storm was there when Peter petitioned Jesus with the request to join Him on the water. The storm was there when Peter leapt from the boat. Peter faltered when he focused more on the storm, and less on the Savior. He started sinking only when he took his eyes off Jesus. Peter's saving grace was in his plea for help. "Lord, save me. And immediately Jesus stretched forth his hand, and caught him" (Matthew 14:30-31).

There is a definite parallel between Peter's actions, and our own lives. The only way we can return to our Father in Heaven is to never take our eyes off Him. He needs to be our constant focus, every day that we walk through this crazy called life, especially during the storms. And in those moments when we struggle, and the winds and waves seem to overtake us, when we feel ourselves sinking, like Peter, all we need to do is look to our Savior and reach for Him. A heartfelt plea of 'Lord, save me' is all we need to remember. That may seem like a daunting, and at times an impossible task, "but his hand is stretched out still."

We often use the mustard seed as an example of how little faith we need in order to receive His help, but it truly doesn't take much faith to plant what can ultimately become a powerful testimony of Jesus Christ. We all have to start somewhere. A quiet prayer just to get through the day, or the hour, even if it's simply 'God, please give me the strength to not strangle another human being'. Get out of your own head and serve others by baking cookies for a friend, and eat two, or five. Find peace in the quiet solitude of a drive in the mountains, a walk around the neighborhood, or hide behind your clothes in the back of the closet. The Savior has promised that his love is available at all times, and in all places, if we sincerely keep him in our sights, and within our reach. President Russell M. Nelson, the Prophet of our church, said it best when he reminded us that, "The Lord does not require perfect faith for us to have access to His perfect power, but He does ask us to believe" ('Christ is Risen; Faith in Him Will Move Mountains'; General Conference, April 2021).

I've thought about the Savior's words in my dream many times, and the messages are just as important today as they were back then. In fact, they are a basic gospel principle that we should always remember. Never take your eyes off the Savior, and not everything is as it seems. So how do we use our gifts and talents to help us stay, or get back on, the covenant path with the Savior in our sights?

A very dear friend of mine once told me that her gift was seeing the little things that God has given us. When she's struggling, she looks for the rainbows during the storm, and not after the rain. She enjoys searching for four leaf clovers instead of grumbling about the weeds; she notices the sweet song of the birds chirping, or the warmth of the sun on her face, instead of focusing on the heat in the middle of a sweltering summer day. She sees the many different types of vegetation that provide natures sweet smelling aroma, the stars in the sky that add light to the darkness, the water in the seas that give us waves to play in, and it reminds her of God's perfect love. She has the divine gift of seeing all the beauty of the earth and she uses that as her foundation to keep her eyes focused on the Savior. And when others are struggling, she lovingly points out the beauty all around as a reminder of God's perfect love for them as well.

If your gift is that of offering prayers, keeping your eyes on the Savior may include expressing gratitude to Heavenly Father for what others deem frivolous, or giving a Priesthood blessing in the middle of the night, or saying a prayer with a friend who is struggling instead of simply offering one. If you are blessed with the gift of healing, then focusing on the Savior may look like providing medical care in low-income areas or third-world countries on mission trips, or sharing your testimony of the gospel when miraculous healing occurs, or holding the hand of a patient as they pass through the veil of mortality. Just as our gifts are individual to each of us, so should be our journey to finding out how to use those gifts to never lose sight of the One bidding us to "Come".

Not only do we need to remember to never take our eyes off the Savior, but we also need to remember that not everything is as it seems. The adversary has perfected the ability to take immoral and ungodly thoughts, actions, choices, and intentions and make them seem acceptable when they most certainly are not. It is only with the help of the Holy Ghost that we can recognize good from evil, truth from lies, otherwise we will see playful dolphins instead of ugly monsters that are just beneath the surface of reality. The gift of discernment is to discern, differentiate, or to perceive by sight or other sense. It means to know or understand through the gift of the Holy Ghost. Elder David A. Bednar taught us that the gift of discernment is:

> A light of protection and direction in a world that grows increasingly dark. You and I can press forward safely and successfully through the mist of darkness and have a clear

sense of spiritual direction. Discernment is so much more than recognizing right from wrong. It helps us distinguish the relevant from the irrelevant, the important from the unimportant, and the necessary from that which is merely nice." (Quick to Observe, BYU devotional, 2006)

Unlike our own personal gifts, the spiritual gift of discernment is given to each of us, but it is only through obedience to the principles of the gospel that we can truly use it to the best of our abilities. We are promised that with this gift, we will not lose our way. We must work to be like those in Lehi's vision of the Tree of Life that when the mist of darkness arose, and they could not see, "they came and caught hold of the end of the rod of iron; and they did press their way forward, continually holding fast to the rod of iron, until they came forth and fell down and partook of the fruit of the tree" (Book of Mormon, 1 Nephi 8:30). Let us all be worthy of the gift of discernment so as not to lose our path in the midst of darkness when not everything is as it seems. May each of us use this gift to keep us from the mundane distractions in life, so that we may never take our eyes off the Savior.

The Lord has promised that when we ask, He will answer; when we reach, He will extend His hand; when we fall, He will help us to stand. "For we know that it is by grace that we are saved, after all we can do" (Book of Mormon, 2 Nephi 25:23). When we find ourselves afraid of the winds, like Peter, we cannot let our fear and doubt allow us to sink. Thankfully, the Atonement has given us the ability to ask for help, and we are guaranteed that the Savior will always reach His hand out to us...but it is up to us to take it. It is up to each of us to use our spiritual gift(s) as an anchor in keeping our eyes on the Savior. Just as the scripture on my rock promises, let us remember "that whosoever believeth in him should not perish, but have everlasting life" (New Testament, John 3:16).

I read a poem titled The Secret that reminded me of Peter's story and my dream. May each of us strive to uncover the secret of how to keep our eyes on the Savior in our own way, with our own God-given gifts and talents. And may we strive to be like my daughter and turn our eyes to Him for comfort.

I MET GOD IN THE MORNING
WHEN MY DAY WAS AT ITS BEST,
AND HIS PRESENCE CAME LIKE SUNRISE
LIKE A GLORY IN MY BREAST.
ALL DAY LONG THE PRESENCE LINGERED,
ALL DAY LONG HE STAYED WITH ME,
AND WE SAILED IN PERFECT CALMNESS
O'ER A VERY TROUBLED SEA.
OTHER SHIPS WERE BLOWN AND BATTERED,
OTHER SHIPS WERE SORE DISTRESSED,
BUT THE WINDS THAT SEEMED TO DRIVE THEM
BROUGHT TO US A PEACE AND REST.
THEN I THOUGHT OF OTHER MORNINGS,
WITH A KEEN REMORSE OF MIND,
WHEN I TOO HAD LOOSED THE MOORINGS,
WITH THE PRESENCE LEFT BEHIND.
SO I THINK I KNOW THE SECRET,
LEARNED FROM MANY A TROUBLED WAY:
YOU MUST SEEK HIM IN THE MORNING
IF YOU WANT HIM THROUGH THE DAY!

From Spiritual Hilltops by Ralph S. Cushman.
Copyright 1932 by Ralph S. Cushman

Chapter 2

"Now you know"

Prayers do not always get answered in the way we expect. In fact, they can come to us in the strangest of ways. I have learned over the years that there is no manual to teach us how God answers our prayers, but rather He personalizes them for our behalf. He knows us individually, and that includes knowing how to get our attention, how to lovingly put us back on the right path, and knowing exactly when and how to answer our prayers in a way that we cannot deny from whom they came.

I started taking the missionary discussions the summer after I graduated high school. My best friend was a member of the church, and it was her influence that first piqued my interest in the gospel, but she was not the only member that I knew. A young man, who had been a friend for several years and lived a few houses down from us, was also a member of the church. He had a bit of a rebellious side and didn't always make the best choices, but I knew his heart was good. He was a year older than I was, and we dated most of my senior year in high school. His family moved out of state shortly after I graduated and we decided that a long-distance relationship was worth the effort, especially since we had started discussing the future. I wanted to surprise him with my newfound interest in the gospel but decided to wait to tell him until I knew, for myself, that it was true.

Shortly before my first semester of college, I agreed to get baptized, and the date was set. I called him, excited to share my news, and yet I also had some anxiety about his reaction, simply because the gospel was not an important part of his life. When I told him that I had been taking the missionary discussions and had set a baptismal date, his response was a disappointingly long sigh. All he said was, "Oh". I ended the conversation shortly thereafter with a heavy heart. I was getting baptized because I knew it was the right thing to do and because it was what I needed in my life. As much as I wanted him to share in my excitement, his reaction did not sway my decision in the slightest. I was saddened, but still determined.

The morning of August 24, 1991, brought an enthusiastic nervousness that I had not felt before. I had a new dress, with new shoes, and my hair styled in a perfect French braid. My best friend's family had arrived with cookies, and the missionaries had the baptismal font ready with warm water. A few talks and musical numbers later, and I took the plunge, so to speak. Covenants were made, the Holy Ghost was confirmed, and I was the newest member of the Church of Jesus Christ of Latter-Day Saints. A small celebration with pictures ended the event, and I went home with a smile on my face and a heart full of joy.

The day ended almost perfectly. Almost. There were a few moments when I felt sadness and disappointment that the young man who I thought loved me, and who was supposed to be excited for me, did not show any interest in my baptism. In fact, he didn't even call to see how things had gone. It bothered me enough that I was starting to doubt our relationship. As much as I wanted to continue dating this young man, my heart was questioning his commitment to me and to the gospel, and I desperately needed guidance from my Heavenly Father. That night before bed, I got down on my knees and said my first heartfelt prayer as a newly baptized member of the church. I pleaded with my Father in Heaven to help me understand my feelings and to guide my thoughts as I looked to my future. As I look back on it now, I'm not entirely sure what I was expecting, but I remember sitting there on my knees for several minutes, waiting for God's reply as though He would simply speak the words aloud for me to hear them. When silence was my only response, and my answer didn't come, I got up off my knees, crawled into bed, quickly fell asleep, and tumbled into a dream.

I was in the hospital, in labor. Labor as in feet-in-the-stirrups, with a sheet draped over me, having contractions, while a doctor stood between my knees telling me to push labor. I was even going through the steps of Lamaze breathing when I heard the words, "You can do it. Keep pushing. I love you. I love you so much." I looked to my left and saw the face of a man I did not recognize. A face that reflected kindness, compassion, understanding and a love so intense that it felt slightly intimidating. But in that moment, I knew that I loved him with just as much intensity, and I realized that it was unconditional for both of us. I also realized that he was my husband and the father of my baby. And the dream ended.

When I woke up the following morning, my very first thought was that my baptism had made me crazy. My second thought was that I had received the answer to my previous night's prayer. I knew that the man in my dream would be the father of my children, and he most assuredly was not the young man I was dating. I promptly sat down with a slightly broken heart and wrote a letter that would end the relationship I had been in for over a year.

A few days later, my best friend called and told me that her brother was coming home from his mission. She asked if I would go with her to the airport to pick him up, and I quickly agreed. I knew and loved her entire family and was excited to have the opportunity to meet her one last brother. As we were standing there at the gate, I remember her bouncing on her toes as the passengers walked by while she impatiently waited to see his face and hug his neck. Several passengers later, a tall, lanky young man wearing a black suit with a missionary name tag and a black Stetson cowboy hat walked off the plane and toward us, and I promptly stopped breathing.

How was I supposed to introduce myself to this young man who owned the face that appeared in my dream a few nights before? "Hi, my name is Sherri, and you don't know it yet, but we're going to get married and have

16

babies someday." Probably not the best idea. Awkward did not even begin to describe how I was feeling at that very moment. I was a recently baptized member, being introduced to a very cute return missionary, in the middle of an airport, after having my prayer answered in the most unlikely and unexpected way. I was flustered, to say the least.

Within a week, we had our first date. Four months later we were engaged. Eight months into our ten-month engagement, I finally told my very cute fiancé about that dream. He was a little shocked, but grateful for the outcome, and slightly relieved that I had kept that secret to myself for so long. That dream was almost 30 years ago, and I still remind my husband that I loved him first.

I was a very impressionable young woman who had become like a small child, kneeling before God, asking for His guidance, and the answer came swiftly and without question. The Savior taught, "Ask, and it shall be given you; seek, and ye shall find; knock, and it shall be opened unto you; for every one that asketh receiveth; and he that seeketh findeth; and to him that knocketh it shall be opened" (New Testament, Matthew 7:7-8). We are also told that, "Whatsoever ye shall ask the Father in my name, which is right, believing that ye shall receive, behold it shall be given unto you" (Book of Mormon, 3 Nephi 18:20). My heart was sincere, and I had faith that my prayer would be heard but was caught off guard in how the answer came. It was a quick lesson to expect the unexpected, and that Heavenly Father does have a sense of humor. Many years later, I would come to realize that it was another example of how God used my spiritual gift to bless my life, and this time it was an answer to a prayer.

God is aware of our needs; He wants to be involved in our lives on a daily basis. We are promised that our prayers are heard, but we are not promised when or how an answer will come. Elder Brook P. Hales stated that:

The Father is aware of us, knows our needs, and will help us perfectly. Sometimes that help is given in the very moment or at least soon after we ask for divine help. Sometimes our most earnest and worthy desires are not answered in the way we hope, but we find that God has greater blessings in store. And sometimes our righteous desires are not granted in this life. (Answers to Prayers; General Conference; April 2019)

Several years ago, shortly after my husband and I married, we were struggling to figure out life, just as most young married couples do. I was in college and pregnant with our first child. My husband battled learning disabilities and had no desire to attend college. We discussed several possibilities including trade schools, the military, and the police force. After a lot of prayer and weighing our options, he decided that he wanted to serve the community as a Highway Patrol officer. This meant he had to pass two tests - a physical test and a written test. He was a runner by nature, and already in great shape, so the physical fitness test was going to be the easiest part of the process. The written test, however, could end up being his nemesis. He researched the requirements and the academy, and we spent hours together studying and memorizing facts to help ensure his success.

The written exam was scheduled first. We said a prayer, and I sent him off with a lot of anxiety on his behalf simply because I knew how his disabilities affected him. A few hours later, he came home with the biggest, sweetest smile on his face. He had passed the written test. Both of us felt that the hardest part was over, and relief set in.

The physical fitness test was scheduled a few days later. This portion required a maximum 10-minute mile, a minimum of 30 sit ups in a minute, and a minimum of 30 pushups in a minute. He cleared the mile in less than six minutes, and he finished with 92 pushups. The end was so close. The timer started for the sit ups and at the 30 second mark, he had completed 27. He only needed 3 more and he would easily pass that portion of the test. It was in that moment that it felt as though someone was literally standing on his chest for those last 30 seconds. He was physically unable to do even one more sit up. The timer ended and he failed the physical fitness portion of the exam.

He should have easily passed. One of his personal gifts is that of strength and physical endurance. God, however, had a different plan and He used my husband's talent of physical strength to intervene during his fitness portion with an obvious, "No" to our prayers. If he had failed the written test, he would have blamed his failure on his disabilities; but in failing the physical test, there was no room for doubt. Both of us knew that God was telling him that being a highway patrol officer wasn't his path to take. We knew this so clearly, we didn't even discuss the possibility of him going back to try again at a later date. Even with God's undeniable answer, we still spent years wondering about the what ifs. What if he had tried again and passed? What if he had passed only to lose his life in service? So many unanswered questions, but both of us knew that God had a plan, and that plan did not include him serving on the police force. That scenario played out 28 years ago. Our paths led us down different roads, and we've been blessed many times over, however that did not stop us from occasionally wondering why he was told no.

Recently, my husband and I were watching a television show based around the police force, and the episode focused on a retired officer who was on a suicide mission after falling victim to the effects of Post-traumatic Stress Disorder (PTSD). In the show, his friends and colleagues were trying to deescalate the situation. The retired officer kept repeating over and over that he was tired of it all and had become just the shell of the man he once was. He simply wanted his mind to shut off so he would stop seeing all the horrors he'd witnessed while on the job. When a commercial came on, I heard my husband whisper quietly, "And that's why I never passed." I turned to him with confusion on my face and responded with,

"Huh?" He said, "The police force. The spirit quietly spoke and said, 'Now you know'. I would have ended up suffering from PTSD and possibly been suicidal at some point, had I ended up on the highway patrol."

Heavenly Father knew how things would have transpired if our prayers had been answered in the way we had wanted. I will always be grateful for the answer of no, and that we were eventually given the answer of why, even if it was 28 years later. It was a much-needed testimony builder that God does hear our prayers and will answer them in His own time. It was also another reminder that answers come by way of our spiritual gifts.

The scriptures are riddled with examples of how, when, and where prayers are answered, but I've often wondered about the spiritual gifts of those receiving their answers. Elizabeth's prayer was to have a child, and she had to wait several years past child-bearing age before she conceived. I wonder if her gift was patience. Or Nephi, whose gift seemed to center around obedience, was blessed with the gold plates after he sought guidance from God, and then strictly obeyed when told to take the life of Laban. When I think of Noah, who was steadfast in the face of mockery for building the ark, I think of the gift of tolerance. Noah was blessed with guidance to build the ark, even while enduring extreme persecution from those whose "every imagination of the thoughts of [his] heart was only evil continually" (Old Testament, Genesis 6:5).

One of our daughters was blessed with the gift of being cheerful, and she owns it. Sometimes annoyingly so. It is a gift that I envy. Even amid her trials, she's happy. Her gift allows her to enjoy life while she's waiting for her answers. And if her answer is no, then she simply shrugs her shoulders, and moves on. She doesn't complain, she doesn't ask why, she doesn't question God, or His timing. Her gift has given her the ability to trust and wait for her prayers to be answered and to be happy in the process.

If your gift is that of speaking in tongues, which does not always mean speaking a foreign language, your prayer may be answered while having a conversation with a friend when you realize that the words being said belong to the spirit and are not your own. Maybe you have the gift of not judging others, and as a result, you are blessed with an abundance of sincere friends who become angels that answer your prayers in a time of need. A few years ago, I was blessed with the opportunity to serve alongside a sister who possesses the gift of genuinely loving others, and her gift is obvious to anyone that knows her. As we visited other members throughout the stake, I was able to witness, firsthand, her prayers being answered as she openly loved and served those within her stewardship.

Life is so much easier when our answers come swiftly and we're given clear direction, but that requires little faith. So how do we endure those times when we are met with silence, or the answer is seemingly not what we wanted or even expected? How can we use our spiritual gifts to recognize and receive those answers that we desperately seek?

If your spiritual gift is that of teaching others, then the obvious answer is to seek for guidance as you prepare a lesson or teach family home evening. But teaching is more than that. It is sharing with friends and family and strangers what you've learned as you recognize God's voice and His answers in the mundane moments of everyday life. Perhaps your gift is looking to God for guidance, in which case accepting the answer of no can come easier, but again, that is the obvious answer. God expects you to do more than simply ask; you must also act. Use your gift of looking to God, then move forward with what your heart desires and let God answer your prayers by leading your steps down the path He has chosen for you.

If you are struggling to know how God can use your gifts to answer your prayers, let me remind you to do as we are taught in the New Testament in Matthew 7:7-8. Reveal your heart's desires and ASK; pray, ponder, study, and put forth mental and spiritual effort as you SEEK; act in faith and follow the promptings you receive as you KNOCK. Our spiritual gifts and talents are not simply given to us to bless the lives of others; they are also one of the many ways God blesses our lives and answers our prayers. My answer came when God used my gift of dreams to provide the guidance I sought, and the answer came immediately. And yet, He used my husband's gift of strength and endurance to put him on a different path altogether but didn't provide the why until many years later. May each of us put forth the effort to have a better understanding of our gift(s) so that we can have greater faith and more easily recognize when God is using our gifts to give us those answers we seek. And let us not forget that in order to receive those answers, we must first use the sacred gift of prayer to ask.

And, perhaps, as those who
do not turn to God in petty trials
will have no habit or such resort
to help them when the great trials come,
so those who have not
learned to ask Him for childish things
will have less readiness to ask Him
for great ones.
We must not be too high-minded.
I fancy we may sometimes be deterred
from small prayers by a sense of
our own dignity rather than God's.

C.S. Lewis, Letters to Malcolm: Chiefly on Prayer; Geoffrey Bles, 1964

Chapter 3

"Mommy, I'm Right Here"

Have you ever lost someone in a public place? A child in a store? A family member at a sporting event? A travel buddy in a strange city? Have you ever felt the fear of not knowing if you'd ever see them again?

Many years ago, our family was vacationing in Disneyland. Our kids wanted to enjoy the dizzying spin of the teacups, so my husband and I escorted them onto the ride and whirled around as fast as we could while the rest of our family watched and waited. The ride ended and just as we were exiting the gate, I looked around, found our family, and headed in their direction, assuming everyone had followed. I turned back around and noticed that our 5-year-old wasn't there. I immediately panicked and started frantically running around looking for her. Thankfully, we discussed this type of situation with our kids beforehand, so she knew to find a Disneyland employee and stay put. Luckily, we found her quickly and the rest of the vacation passed without incident, but I never wanted to experience that kind of fear, ever again.

My husband and I started our family when we were quite young. At the age of 25, I had been married for six years, and we had three babies under the age of 5. Due to complications from my first delivery, and the toll that having babies takes on some women's bodies, my doctor informed me that I should seriously consider not having any more children. I did not argue with that suggestion, and we made the decision to permanently prevent additional pregnancies. My husband and I both felt that our family was complete. It would be several years later, after a dream that took me by complete surprise, that our feelings of completeness would be doubted and questioned to the point of near desperation.

In the dream, I was anxiously running through the empty halls of our church building, desperately searching for someone, but I did not know who that someone was. My fear was quickly escalating into a sheer panic as I ran around looking in every room, only to find them all empty. I finally came to the nursery room and threw open the door. There, sitting on a yellow and green Little Tikes slide was a beautiful, brown-haired girl, dressed in white. I remember relief washing over me that I had finally found this beautiful child, and after catching my breath, said "Honey, where have you been? Mommy has been looking all over for you. It scared me when I couldn't find you." She simply replied in the sweetest voice, "Mommy, I'm right here, waiting for you." And the dream ended.

The panic I felt when looking for that little girl in my dream was just as real as the panic I felt when desperately searching for our daughter in a gigantic theme park packed with thousands of people. Even though it felt as though I had another little girl waiting for me to find her, there was nothing I could do about it.

I spent several months trying to convince my husband that we needed to either start the adoption process, or I was going to surgically undo my sterilization because my little girl was waiting, patiently. He, however, did not feel the same. We were at an impasse and neither of us was willing to budge.

Finally, one evening during dinner with friends, my husband proceeded to tell us of a dream he had had the previous night. In his dream, he was standing in the foyer at our church building after sacrament meeting, chatting with friends before we all left to go home. He stated that a little brown-haired girl, dressed in white, ran up to him and said "Daddy, hold me." He proceeded to pick her up, and we left for home shortly thereafter. Her name was Isabella.

I sat in stunned silence.

My little girl, the one for whom I had been fighting for, for months, was not just a dream any longer. She was real, and she was waiting for me, and her name was Isabella. My husband could no longer deny what I had known for quite a while.

I immediately started researching all our options and quickly came to realize that because of other medical issues, sterilization reversal was not possible. I could not carry another child and my heart sank, but not all was lost.

We considered having a surrogate mother and even discussed it with our bishop to ensure it was not against church policy. After receiving confirmation that it was acceptable, and before we even discussed it with others, a small miracle occurred when we had a friend volunteer to carry our child. I was elated. We hired an attorney, drew up paperwork to ensure privacy and protection for all of us, created a timeline and moved forward with the thought of our Isabella becoming a reality, until our surrogate changed her mind in the last hour. My heart was utterly broken, but again, not all was lost.

During the months we spent working with our intended surrogate, I had not given up on researching other options. I had already logged hundreds of hours investigating the laws, processes and costs associated with stateside and international adoption. After a lot of fasting, prayers, temple visits and discussions within our family, we were led to seek the help of the professionals at the LDS Family Services adoption center. We met with a social worker, had our consultation, and attended the temple one last time to make doubly sure that we were walking the path that God had intended us to walk. During that visit to the temple, both my husband and I received an undeniable sacred confirmation that our Isabella was waiting for us and that we were most definitely on the right path. I was consumed with a combination of peace, determination, and excitement.

Shortly thereafter, we began the long and daunting process of completing our adoption home study, which is required by law before any child(ren) can be placed in a home. A home study consists of multiple interviews, home visits by the social worker, pages and pages of paperwork including financials, education, personal and family medical history, parenting essay questions, and finally creating an in-depth family profile. After several anxiety filled months, our home study was approved, and we were ready for Isabella to join our family. We were finally able to breathe a sigh of relief and at that point, all we had to do was wait, so that's what we did. We waited on Heavenly Father to answer our prayers. And we waited. And waited some more.

Two very long years passed, and we were terribly discouraged thinking God had forgotten us. Then, two days before Christmas, we were given another small miracle. Our social worker called and said that our family had been chosen by a mother living in Atlanta. She wanted to meet our entire family and not just my husband and I, which caused me to be cautiously optimistic. My whole soul yearned for things to work out, and I wanted our kids to be a part of the process, but my momma heart had anxiety about the possibility of their little hearts getting broken. In an effort to trust in God's plan, we packed overnight bags, piled into our van, and headed down to Atlanta to meet a stranger carrying what we prayed would be our Isabella.

Our birth mom was a beautiful, young 19-year-old, with two little boys, ages 5 and 10 months, and was 7 months pregnant. She was struggling in all aspects of her life and could not financially or emotionally afford to care for another baby. The dinner meeting went very well, and we all drove back home, excitedly talking about how things went, and what our future would look like as a family of six. Our children were invested at this point, and with each passing day, they grew more and more anxious to meet their new bundle of joy.

As the due date drew near, we were informed that the physician had agreed to a scheduled induction so that my husband and I would be present for the birth of our little one. The date was set for a Monday morning. Arrangements were made for our children to stay and attend school, and my husband and I were packed and ready to go. We kissed our littles goodbye, put them on the school bus, and then we loaded up our van with all the baby necessities. I grabbed my purse and was headed out the door when my cell phone rang. It was our social worker whom I assumed was calling to wish us safe travels. I could not have been more wrong.

I cheerfully answered the phone and was immediately met with a quivering voice. For the next several minutes, I once again sat in stunned silence, as our social worker proceeded to inform me that our birth mom had delivered a little girl two days prior, and she decided to keep the baby. My heart shattered into a million tiny pieces. My world was turned upside down. My foundation was shaken. My eyes cried countless tears. How were we going to tell our children that their baby was not coming home? How was I going to emotionally move on, knowing my sweet, beautiful Isabella, was once again only a dream? That entire day was one of the worst days of my life, and in that moment, it truly did feel like all was lost.

We decided to put our adoption status on hold temporarily until we could make a decision that was not solely based on emotions. After several weeks, and more fasting, prayer, and temple attendance, we decided as a family to permanently withdraw from the adoption process. It was a painful decision to make, but one we felt was best for us. Even though my heart was shattered, I felt a calming peace that only the Savior can bring in a moment of great sadness and despair.

Many years have gone by since that heartbreaking situation and I still think about our Isabella quite often. I also think about the whys. So many whys. Why did I see that little girl in my dream? Why was it also confirmed with my husband? Why was in confirmed, in the temple of all places, that we were supposed to move forward with the adoption? Why did my children have to experience such heartache? And why, why, why were we allowed to fall in love with a little girl that would never be a part of our family?

It took me a long time to have the emotional strength to speak about my Isabella. Even now, my heart still has a hole that will not be filled in this life. It has also taken me many years to understand only a few of the lessons I learned from that experience, with the most significant being simple obedience. In truth, I do not know any of the answers to my many questions of why, other than it was what God had asked me to do. I often feel like a child whose parent says, 'because I said so,' but I know that God does not work that way. I know He has a plan. I trust that I will know the answers in His time. And I believe that Isabella is still there, waiting patiently, for her turn to come to this earth and fulfill what I can only assume is a great and wonderful calling.

Yes, my heart was broken, but more importantly, I walked the path that God asked me to walk, and I did it with faith. The end result was not what I expected, or even wanted, but it was a defining moment in my life of the importance of obedience. We may never know the why's behind what we're asked to do, but as long as we're willing to walk the walk, we will be blessed in the end. Elder L. Tom Perry once said that "Obedience is a choice. It is a choice between our own limited knowledge and power, and God's unlimited wisdom and omnipotence" ('Obedience Through Our Faithfulness'; General Conference, April 2014).

Any time I start doubting my own ability to be obedient, I am reminded of the 116 lost pages to the Book of Mormon. In 1 Nephi, chapter 9, Nephi was commanded to make two sets of records, and because of his obedience, he did so without question. Verses 5-6 state, "Wherefore, the Lord hath command me to make these plates for a wise purpose in him, which purpose I know not. But the Lord knoweth all things from the beginning; wherefore, he prepareth a way to accomplish all his works among the children of men; for behold, he hath all power unto the fulfilling of all his words" (1 Nephi 9:5-6). Then, 985 years later, Mormon was working on the abridgement of the small and large plates, and he had hundreds of pages and stories to choose from as he was compiling it all. But again, Mormon was prompted to include both records. Why include two of the same stories when he had so many other options? But again, Mormon was obedient to the promptings of the spirit when he said:

Wherefore, I chose these things, to finish my record upon them, which remainder of my record I shall take from the plates of Nephi; and I cannot write the hundredth part of the things of my people. But behold, I shall take these plates, which contain these prophesyings and revelations, and put them with the remainder of my record And I do this for a wise purpose; for thus it whispereth me, according to the workings of the Spirit of the Lord which is in me. And now, I do not know all things; but the Lord knoweth all things which are to come; wherefore, he worketh in me to do according to his will. (Words of Mormon 1:5-7)

Fast forward another 1,443 years to when Joseph Smith was translating the Book of Mormon. With Martin Harris as his scribe, Joseph Smith had successfully translated the Book of Lehi, or the first 116 pages, which consisted of Lehi's dreams, his prophecies and his teachings. Martin's family did not believe that Joseph Smith was a prophet and as a result, Martin requested to take the translated pages as proof of the work they had done. Joseph went to God and asked for permission and was immediately told no. Martin was obstinate regarding his request and Joseph asked twice more. Finally, permission was granted, with specific instructions on how those pages were to be handled. Unfortunately, because of simple disobedience to those instructions, Martin Harris lost that sacred manuscript a short time later.

Until the lost pages are found, or we receive additional revelation as to the content of those records, we will never know exactly what was contained within those pages. We do, however, have what Nephi added, and then what Mormon included, as part of what was missing. Nephi obeyed and added a second account of his father's teachings, including Lehi's vision of the Tree of Life. Mormon obeyed and included both accounts in his abridgement. And neither of them would learn in their mortal life the significance of following the promptings of the Holy Ghost. It is because of their obedience that we have some of what was lost on those 116 pages. It is because of their obedience that Heavenly Father was able to compensate for the lack of discretion on the part of Joseph Smith and Martin Harris.

I may not know until I am on the other side of the veil why God used my gift to put me on a path that would seem to only bring sadness and heartache, but I have faith that knowledge will come eventually. One of my favorite scriptures to turn to when doubting God's will is found in Doctrine and Covenants 58:3 which states, "Ye cannot behold with our natural eyes, for the present time, the design of your God concerning those things which shall come hereafter, and the glory which shall follow after much tribulation." Being denied the opportunity to have Isabella join our family is the definition of 'much tribulation', but I trust in the miracle of God's love and the 'glory which shall follow'.

One of my closest friends has lived in the beautiful state of Tennessee for several years, and she has always considered it her home, so much so that she never wanted to live anywhere else. She raised her children there. Her friends were there, her memories were there, her heart was there, and her future was there, or so she thought. A few years ago, her and her husband sold their home and decided to spend a few months with family in Utah in the interim, until definite plans were made for their future in Tennessee. Three months turned into six months, which turned into nine months, which turned into a year. She was still in Utah and desperately longed to be back in her home state of Tennessee. Much to her dismay, opportunities were presented that would keep her and her husband in Utah for an unforeseen amount of time. She was heartbroken, but she maintained her faith that God would soon take her back home, however that would not come to pass. This amazing woman has the gift of not only deeply understanding the sacred covenants she made in the temple, but her gift also encompasses a profound sense of responsibility in her divine role as wife and mother. God used her gift as a means of helping her to support her husband and accept changes in her life that she may not have otherwise accepted. And once she opened herself up to the promptings she received through her gift and began to walk her own personal path of obedience, her heart began to change, and she could more easily recognize the tender mercies that came from trusting in her Heavenly Father.

Like my story of obedience, and the many stories that can be found in the scriptures, this sister may never know why she was taken from her home in Tennessee and transplanted to Utah, but she has the faith to know that God's plan is divine and that she will be blessed for her obedience, even if it comes without understanding. Elder Jeffrey R. Holland beautifully said:

The tests of life are tailored for our own best interests, and all will face the burdens best suited to their own mortal experience. In the end we will realize that God is merciful as well as just and that all the rules are fair. We can be reassured that our challenges will be the ones we needed and conquering them will bring blessings we could have received in no other way. ('What I Wish Every New Member Knew – And Every Longtime Member Remembered'; Ensign, October 2006)

Allowing God to use our gifts to help us learn obedience is not an easy task. If it were, everyone would be doing it. So, what does that look like if

31

you have the gift of sharing your testimony? Maybe you will be called on a mission, like Samuel the Lamanite, and will be asked to cry repentance and share your testimony with those who are lost. You may be mocked, and it may be difficult, and you may wonder why you are asked to do such a hard task but do it anyway. If you have the gift of patience, you may be blessed with a child or children, either through pregnancies or adoptions or both, who have physical, mental, or emotional needs that requires constant guidance and direction. Parenting them may be hard and exhausting, but your obedience to His will and calling upon your heavenly gift will allow you to walk the path that He has prepared you for. Maybe your gift is that of seeing the good in everyone, but you experience extreme heartache because of the actions of another. Knowing that they are a child of God and looking for the good that may be buried deep within them, may feel like an unreachable and impossible task while in the depths of your sorrow. You may want to question God's urging when you are prompted to use the Atonement to strengthen your gift by searching for their goodness, but trust in Him and your obedience will bring a comfort that only the Son of God can give.

Each of us is given a gift(s) of the spirit, and each of us will be faced with burdens and trials that seem unbearable. Our gifts may take us down paths that we do not wish to travel, but if we are obedient and we walk in faith, keeping our eyes on God with an eternal perspective, then those same gifts can be merciful blessings in the end.

I struggled with not having the opportunity to physically hold and love on our Isabella, but what I did not know at the time was that God would be merciful and would eventually allow her to make another appearance in the future. I cannot help but smile, knowing that she may be only a dream for now, but that won't last forever. One day I will be given the opportunity to love on her and what a sweet sacred moment that will be. Just as my friend still struggles with the desire to move back to her home state, she also has the faith to be obedient, knowing that someday she'll know why she was asked to make that sacrifice, even if that answer doesn't come until the next life. Our journey will not be easy, but may we be insightful enough to allow our gifts to teach us obedience, even when we do not see the results with our mortal eyes. And may we always strive to follow the words of the hymn 'I'll Go Where You Want Me to Go' which states:

It may not be on the mountain height,

Or over the stormy sea,

It may not be at the battle's front,

My Lord will have need of me.

But if, by a still, small voice he calls,

To paths that I do not know,

I'll answer, dear Lord, with my hand in thine:

I'll go where you want me to go.

Perhaps today there are loving words

Which Jesus would have me speak;

There may be now in the paths of sin

Some wand'rer whom I should seek

O Savior, if thou wilt be my guide,

Tho dark and rugged the way,

My voice shall echo the message sweet:

I'll say what you want me to say.

There's surely somewhere a lowly place

In earth's harvest fields so wide

Where I may labor through life's short day

For Jesus, the Crucified.

So trusting my all to thy tender care,

And knowing thou lovest me,

I'll do thy will with a heart sincere:

I'll be what you want me to be.

I'll go where you want me to go dear Lord,

Over mountain or plain or sea;

I'll say what you want me to say dear Lord;

I'll be what you want me to be.

Mary Brown; "I'll Go Where You Want Me to Go"; Church of Jesus Christ of Latter-Day Saints Hymnal # 270

Chapter 4

"I Already Told You"

Doubt. A feeling of uncertainty or lack of conviction. To fear or to be afraid. To be skeptical of God's word or His plan. To be unbelieving. To lose even a small amount of faith.

We've all been there. Even some of the greatest prophets in the scriptures have doubted. Thomas was a disciple of Christ who walked with Him, who sat at His feet and learned from the Savior himself. Thomas was present when Jesus taught the gospel, he saw the miracles performed by the Savior's hands, and he knew that Jesus was the Son of God. And yet, when others tried to convince him of the Savior's resurrection, he responded with "except I shall see in his hands the print of the nails and put my finger into the print of the nails, and thrust my hand into his side, I will not believe" (New Testament, John 2.:25). Lehi expressed his frustrations when Nephi accidentally broke his bow and returned to camp without food but was later "brought down into the depths of sorrow" for his moment of doubt (Book of Mormon, 1 Nephi 16:25). And then there's Moses from the Old Testament. Moses who led the Israelites from captivity. Moses who parted the Red Sea. Moses who gave us the 10 Commandments and the Mosaic Law. Moses.

When Moses fled Egypt and the Pharaoh who sought to take his life, he was 40 years of age. He ended up in a town called Midian where he became a humble shepherd, met his wife, started a family, and was perfectly content with his situation. Over the next 40 years, Moses was taught the gospel by his father-in-law Jethro, the Midian priest, who also ordained him with the Melchizedek Priesthood. In short, Jethro helped prepare Moses to lead the Israelite exodus, prophesy of the coming of the Savior, and enact the Mosaic Law. Yet Moses doubted. He didn't doubt once or twice. He didn't even stop doubting after three, four, or five times. Moses doubted the Lord seven different times. Seven. Regardless, the

Lord remained patient and continued to encourage him on his journey to greatness.

We read of Moses' lack of faith in Exodus chapters 3 through 7 and learn that he didn't waste any time in expressing his apprehension from the very onset. When God initially commanded Moses to return to Egypt to rescue His people, Moses asked, "Who am I, that I should go unto Pharaoh" (3:11)? God's reply was simple. "Certainly I will be with thee" (3:12). Moses pushed back and said, "they [the Israelites] will not believe me, nor harken unto my voice: for they will say, The Lord has not appeared unto thee" (4:1). In an effort to reassure Moses and move things along, the Lord proved Himself by turning Moses's rod into a serpent, He caused Moses' hand to become leprous, and He turned the water from the river to blood upon the sand (4:2-9). At this point, one would think that Moses had seen enough to believe in the power from above. And yet, the doubts and excuses continued.

Moses' response, even after witnessing multiple miracles by the hand of the Lord, was, "I am not eloquent I am slow of speech, and of a slow tongue", meaning Moses had a speech impediment (4:10). Even still, the Lord remained patient when He responded with, "Who hath made man's mouth? Or who maketh the dumb, or deaf, or seeing, or the blind? Have not I the Lord? Now therefore go, and I will be with thy mouth, and teach thee what thou shalt say" (4:11-12). Remember I said that Moses doubted seven times? Immediately after the Lord reminded Moses that He was the creator of man and would bless him with the ability to speak, Moses, yet again, dug in his heels. "And he said, O my Lord, send, I pray thee, by the hand of him whom thou wilt send" (4:13). In other words, can't you send someone else? Am I the only one that looks back and cringes at the number of times I've said those exact same words? Can't you send someone else? And poor Moses. He finally crossed the line that none of us want to cross, because the very next words spoken were said by an extremely exacerbated Lord. "And the anger of the Lord was kindled against Moses and he said, Is not Aaron the Levite thy brother? I know that he can speak well. And thou shalt speak unto him, and put words in his mouth: and I will be with thy mouth, and with his mouth, and will teach you what ye shall do" (4:14-15). Moses angered the Lord, and yet He showed mercy to Moses in his time of need, as is His way. Moses did not escape the mission he was called to do and was still required to travel to Egypt to free the Lord's people from Pharaoh, but the Lord blessed him with a mouthpiece to ease his anxiety.

Fast forward to when Moses made it into Egypt and requested that Pharaoh release the people. Pharaoh denies Moses' request and in retaliation, Pharaoh places an even greater burden upon the slaves. Moses goes back to the Lord, once again questioning His plan and purpose when he said, "Lord, wherefore has thou so evil entreated this people? Why is it that thou hast sent me? For since I came to Pharaoh to speak in thy name, he hath done evil to this people; neither has thou delivered thy people at all" (5:22-23). How often do we try our best to be obedient in God's eyes, and yet, the situation and the burden seems harder than before? Do we go back and ask why? Do we murmur because of the expectation that being obedient is supposed to bring blessings? Do we ask "why is it thou hast sent me?" And God's reply to us, like unto Moses, is not always what we want to hear. "Wherefore say unto the children of Israel, I am the Lord, and I will bring you out from under the burdens of the Egyptians" (5:6). God did not say when the burden would be lifted. God did not say how it would come to pass. And God certainly did not say it would be easy. God only reminded Moses of the promise that it would happen and simply told him to go and do.

Moses, seemingly in an impossible situation, questions God further. "Behold, the children of Israel have not hearkened unto me; how then shall Pharaoh hear me" (6:12)? A legitimate question, but a doubt filled one, nonetheless. How could Moses expect Pharaoh to heed his words when his own people weren't listening? "And the Lord spake unto Moses and unto Aaron and gave them a charge to bring the children of Israel out of the land of Egypt" (6:13). Again, no explanations. No excuses. Just do it. And Moses is keenly aware that Pharaoh knows of his speech impediment and complains once more about it when he says, "Behold, I am of uncircumcised lips, and how shall Pharaoh hearken unto me" (7:1)? The Lord answers Moses with the same short response. "I have made thee a god to Pharaoh: and Aaron thy brother shall be thy prophet. Thou shalt speak all that I command thee: and Aaron thy brother shall speak unto Pharaoh, that he send the children of Israel out of his land."

So many instances of doubt. Not once did God give Moses a step-by-step instruction manual on how to lead the children of Israel out of Egypt; he simply said go and do. And Moses finally went and did. He obeyed without further argument, and the plan began to move forward. Shortly thereafter, Egypt was stricken with the ten plagues because of Pharaoh's refusal to obey God's commands.

God gave Moses plenty of chances to obey and was patient when he doubted. God gave Pharaoh plenty of chances to obey and was patient in his refusals. And God gives us plenty of chances to obey and is patient in our doubts, and in our refusals, but like Moses, God's patience only goes so far.

I often wonder how frustrated God gets with me in my persistence to not do things He has asked of me. Or the amount of patience He has when I worry about the future or continue to ask for answers on how, when and why? And then I remember a few of the dreams I've had, and I quickly try to move from worry to faith, but sometimes that's harder than it seems.

Several years ago, our son was in a relationship that caused me a lot of anxiety. He and his girlfriend had broken some of our most basic house rules and after reminding him of our expectations, a wedge began to grow between us and him. Shortly thereafter, he moved out and moved in with his girlfriend. Over time, his visits back home became less frequent until we saw him only on holidays, and he and his girlfriend usually showed up late and then left early. Even during those short periods of time they were in our home, it was evident that my son and his girlfriend did not get along. The relationship was clearly unhealthy, but in order to not cause more angst between us, we said nothing and only loved them. However, that did not stop me from worrying excessively. That is until one morning, as I was coming out of a deep sleep, I heard the words "She does not love him." No pictures, no vision, no scene, just a simple statement of fact. In that moment, I knew exactly who was speaking, and who He was speaking about. A sense of relief and sadness washed over me. I knew that the relationship would eventually end, but what would the emotional cost be to our son who had made major life decisions based on his relationship with this girl.

Days turned into weeks, weeks turned into months, and nothing had changed in regard to their relationship. A few years later, after a planned weekend to the beach with her family, they came back engaged. My anxiety skyrocketed. After learning that she was no longer his girlfriend but now his fiancé, I immediately remembered my dream and got angry. I remember asking Heavenly Father, "Why"? Why did you tell me she didn't love him if they were going to get married? Why would you let this relationship continue if it's going to end anyway? Why did you ease my anxiety for it to end up ten times worse? Why? I was acting just as Moses had. After a few weeks of stewing in my own soupy mess of restless uncertainty (no doubt God was sitting back watching me have a temper tantrum), I was rewarded with yet another visionless, pictureless, colorless statement. Again, in the morning twilight, He clearly and sternly said, "I already told you; she doesn't love him." Ouch.

I woke up feeling like a badly misbehaved child. His voice was hard yet patient. Booming but soft and kind. I felt chastised and loved. All at the same time. And then I remembered, faith precedes the miracle. I must have faith, even that of a mustard seed, before God can work miracles in my life. While I am glad it did not take me seven times to question the Lord, as it did Moses, I did need to gain that testimony of trusting Him. And trust Him I did. Every time I worried about our son, I was brought back to those stinging words...I already told you. It was several months later when that relationship came to an abrupt end. I never again want to watch one of my children endure such a painful trial, however our son learned many important lessons and is now in a much better place in life.

It's part of human nature to worry. We worry about our marriages, family relationships, finances, employment, medical illnesses, our future, our choices. And we worry about those same things in the lives of those we love. And worry, stress or anxiety is not always a bad thing; for there must be opposition in all things. Even Jacob worried about his people when he said, "but I this day am weighed down with much more desire and anxiety for the welfare of your souls than I have hitherto been. For behold, as yet, ye have been obedient unto the word of the Lord, which I have given unto you" (Book of Mormon, Jacob 2:3-4). His people had been doing what they were asked to do, but he still worried. We all worry. We all doubt.

I have since gained a stronger testimony of trusting my Heavenly Father, but that does not mean I don't stumble every now and again. I am only human, as are we all. Doubting is part of growing and learning to have faith. Regardless of your spiritual gift(s), God will give you the answers that you need, when you need them. And sometimes those answers are not step-by-step instructions, but simply, go and do. Sometimes those answers are simple statements with no explanation. Regardless of the subject of your doubt or anxiety, always remember that God has you in the palm of His hands. Do you love to read? You may question a prompting to pick up and read what would seem to be a dreary book that does not interest you in the least. Read it anyway. Do you have the gift of learning? You may become frustrated when the spirit urges you to go back to school or take a class that has nothing to do with your major.

Take the class anyway. Do you have the gift of asking others for help? Then it may seem confusing when you are guided to seek assistance on a matter that could easily be done on your own. Ask anyway.

This may sound strange, but I honestly feel like Moses' gift was that of faith. Yes, he doubted, several times, but look who he became! He was given the gift of faith but was not expected to be perfect at it. He was given the gift and then Heavenly Father taught him how to use it through trial and error. Could God have stopped the doubts in the beginning? Absolutely. Would Moses have gained a testimony strong enough to part the Red Sea had he not questioned the Lord over, and over, and over again? Probably not.

Just as Moses needed reminding from time to time, do not get discouraged when you hear those loving words, "I already told you." Practice allows us the ability to understand our gifts better, and in turn we will be better able to use them as God intends. The more times you overcome your doubts, the greater your capacity to believe in God's plan. Jeffrey R. Holland said that all we must do is "Hold fast to what you already know and stand strong until additional knowledge comes. You have more faith than you think you do." And this brings me to my second example.

Similar to our first situation, my husband and I struggled with having to watch a loved one make choices in contrast to everything they knew to be true. Married in the temple and sealed for time and all eternity, then divorced. Covenants broken, promises unkept. It hurt my heart terribly and I often wondered where their path would lead. And God gave me the tiniest nibble of eternity. And this time it was an actual dream.

We were all standing outside the doors of the temple, waiting for the newly sealed couple to emerge. And there she was. Holding hands with the one she loved, arms raised high in celebration, and my heart exploded with happiness. I could feel her joy. I could see her spirit shine through

41

the smile on her face. And then the dream ended. I remember waking up wanting to jump for joy, but I was also caught in a moment of confusion. While I clearly saw this beautiful young woman, I could not see who she married. And that was slightly frustrating. I knew his height, hair color, and body type, but not his face. I also knew that when the day came that she introduced us to him, I would know immediately that God's plan was in motion.

And true to how things happen in life, additional decisions were made that caused me quick moments of worry on her behalf, however, I never allowed those doubts to linger, learning from my previous experience. I did not want to hear the words "I already told you", ever again. But God is merciful, and loving, and patient, and kind, and all things good. And several months later, He gave me part two of that scenario when in my second dream, the lovely, beautiful girl was waiting for her young man to get done playing baseball, and this time she said his name. I was a bit shocked then, and I am still shocked now when I take the time to think about it. In all honesty, it makes me laugh knowing that God truly does have a sense of humor. And regardless of where she is in her life at any given time, I will never doubt that God has her in the palm of his hand as well. I still have no idea how that scene will play out, but I look forward to the day it happens because what I won't do is doubt.

In those times of doubt, focus on your gift(s). Think about how God can, and will, use them to ease your anxiety, help you build up your trust in Him, and answer your pleas for help. He may not give you a play-by-play synopsis of how things will work out, but again, faith precedes the miracle. And never forget that mastering a gift does not happen overnight and can only be achieved as we stumble and fall short, with Heavenly Father there to pick us up and dust us off. Hearing Him say, "I told you so," isn't always a joyous occasion, but let's be grateful that Heavenly Father loves us enough to be patient, and that He will send us those reminders when we need them. It took me over forty years to even begin

42

to get a grasp on my gift, and I still get it wrong, but God is merciful and patient with me, as He is with everyone, always.

May we strive to not doubt seven times. May we work harder to not get frustrated when bows are broken. May we not require signs but rather have the faith to believe in the One who owns the prints of the nails, and who holds us in the palm of His hands. And may we strive to choose our faith over our doubts, in every situation.

"The Savior is never closer to you than when you are facing or climbing a mountain with faith."

Russell M. Nelson, "Christ is Risen; Faith in Him Will Move Mountains"; General Conference, April 2021

Chapter 5

"Please, Forgive Me"

March 22, 1933. After World War II had ended, Hitler set up the first concentration camp in German-occupied Poland as detention centers for those who opposed the Nazi regime. One particular camp held a man who was believed to be a newly incarcerated prisoner. It was later discovered that the man in question had been held for over 6 years, which seemed impossible given that he had not become weak and emaciated. The prisoners later learned that their fellow survivor was a Polish father and lawyer who was kept alive due to his knowledge and ability to translate languages. After further inquiries, they were told that the German soldiers had invaded his hometown and proceeded to line up his wife, his two daughters, and his three sons, killing them all with machine gun fire, as he watched, horrified at the sight. When asked about it, the loving husband and father responded with:

> I had to decide right then whether or not to let myself hate the soldiers who had done this. It was an easy decision, really. I was a lawyer. In my practice I had seen what hate could do to people's minds and bodies. Hate had just killed the six people who mattered most to me in the world. I decided then that I would spend the rest of my life – whether it was a few days or many years – loving every person I came in contact with." (George G. Ritchie with Elizabeth Sherrill, Return from Tomorrow, Waco, Texas: Chosen Books, 1978, p. 116.)

December 31, 1948. The cry of a newborn baby girl could be heard down the hall in the hospital in Phoenix, Arizona. Much to her parent's unease, this beautiful little one was born with a cleft lip and palate, a genetic birth defect where the baby's lip and mouth palate do not form completely, leaving an opening in the lip and roof of the mouth. The long-term effects of this disorder would be a struggle through her entire

44

childhood and young adult years, even up to and including her twenties. Speech impediments, hearing issues, eating and drinking difficulties, and multiple surgeries were just a few of the trials that the actual defect would cause. To make matters worse, her burdens were amplified by having to tolerate gawking from adults, being made fun of and bullied by children at school, and feeling isolated and alone because no one understood how she felt. These outside cruelties would have been enough for anyone to lose hope, but she had another trial in her life that was more difficult than all the others combined; her father was an abusive alcoholic. It was not uncommon for him to spat things like, "you're so ugly, no one will ever love you", or make fun of the lisp that the cleft lip had caused, or smack her around while telling her he didn't want a freak for a daughter. The mental, physical, and emotional abuse she suffered at the hands of her father was worse than the physical deformities she was born with. Her relationship with him was strained, at best, for most of her adult life. It wasn't until he was in his late seventies and alone that he finally took the steps to get sober. He only had a few years left of his troubled life and needed help. His daughter, who simply wanted a father's love, was first in line to care for the elderly man. She attended to his needs, serving him until the day he died. It was during this period of time that she found forgiveness for all he had done and said to her in her younger years and focused on appreciating the few years they shared together.

October 5, 2012. Sara married Jeff, her very best friend, after a whirlwind romance full of love and laughter. The morning of their wedding was sunny and bright and warm, and a beautiful representation of what their family would symbolize: eternity. Life was perfect for Sara and Jeff, and full of limitless possibilities. Both of them looked forward to a long happy life together; that is until February 17, 2013, a measly 4 months later, when, in the early morning hours of Jeff returning home from work, he was killed by a drunk driver. Sara's world abruptly stopped moving forward. The loss came first, then the pain, and then the anger. What was a future without her best friend to share it with? What would her hopes and dreams look like without the love of her life by her side? How would she ever have the strength to move forward in a world without Jeff in it? Days turned into weeks. Weeks turned into months. Sara found herself at a crossroads as she walked into the courthouse to attend the sentencing hearing of the individual who had killed her husband. With strength and grace that only God could provide, Sara stood in front of the judge, offering forgiveness, and plead for leniency in the sentencing of the man that had taken the life of the one she loved. Sara later wrote, "The grace I have accessed from my Savior has changed my life. I've learned to forgive and love, even when it hurt. The Savior's grace pushed me to want to be something different than my anger. His grace has healed me."

All three of these stories speak of strength in offering forgiveness. There are unending examples that can be found in the everyday lives of others and the courage it takes to find that forgiveness. Each of us will face difficult situations that require forgiving another, whether it be due to an intentional act or unintentional carelessness. And at some point, that forgiveness may seem to be an impossible task, but try to remember what the scriptures tell us. "Ye ought to forgive one another; for he that forgiveth not his brother his trespasses standeth condemned before the Lord; for there remaineth in him the greater sin. I, the Lord, will forgive whom I will forgive, but of you it is required to forgive all men" (Doctrine and Covenants 64:9-10). The reminder comes again in Matthew to "Love your enemies, bless them that curse you, do good to them that hate you, and pray for them which despitefully use you, and persecute you" (New Testament, Matthew 5:44). And then the unfathomable words spoken by our Savior, after being beaten and tortured, then nailed to a cross, "Father, forgive them; for they know not what they do" (New Testament, Luke 23:34).

During the Savior's ministry and while teaching His disciples, Peter asked a very poignant question when he said, "Lord, how oft shall my brother sin against me, and I forgive him? Till seven times?" Assuming

Peter felt that seven times was quite liberal for one to be expected to forgive another, I'm sure he was shocked when the Savior's response was, "I say not unto thee, Until seven times: but, Until seventy times seven" (Matthew 18:21-22). George Herbert, a 5th century poet, wisely stated, "He that cannot forgive others breaks the bridge over which he himself must pass if he would ever reach heaven; for everyone has need to be forgiven."

Conference talks, recorded devotionals, scripture stories, and even primary lessons on the process of how to forgive are readily available to anyone who seeks to learn about this very basic gospel principle. Setting the example and encouraging others to forgive, teaching about the peace that comes from letting the hurt go and promising the eternal benefits of allowing the atonement to work in our lives, is often what we hear most about. But what of those who need to be forgiven?

Did the German soldiers ever seek forgiveness from the Polish father whose wife and children were slain? Did the father ever tell his daughter he was wrong for the many years of abuse she endured at his hand? Did the drunk driver apologize to the widow of the man he killed? And if they didn't follow through on the requirements of the plan of repentance, how would it affect their eternal salvation? Elder James E. Talmage teaches us in *Jesus, The Christ,* that "to forgiveness man may set no bounds; the forgiveness, however, must be merited by the recipient." In short, we, as the ones offering forgiveness are not to set boundaries on the number of times we forgive, nor are we to create conditions in which forgiveness is necessitated. We simply are to forgive. However, Talmage also points out that the one needing forgiveness must be worthy of it, which worthiness is only granted by our Savior alone. Whether others are worthy of forgiveness is not for us to determine; our job, the commandment we are given, is to forgive.

Many years ago, I made a mistake. I committed a sin that broke my own heart. But only the Lord and I knew about it. I did my due diligence in asking for His forgiveness and went about my life, and I was truly sorry. Deep down I was ashamed. But every now and then, I would get the nagging feeling that I needed to seek the forgiveness of the one that I had secretly deceived. I told myself, many times, that I would rather die with my secret than to hurt someone I love by admitting my guilt. It wasn't anything that needed a Bishop's intervention, but for me, it was the worst kind of betrayal. The guilt began to fester until one day, I pled with my Heavenly Father to take the guilt away. And of course, He answered my prayer in a way that made me realize I could wait no longer keep my secret. He lovingly showed me what would happen if I didn't own up to my mistake.

In my dream, I was looking down on the scene that was taking place before me. The abusive alcoholic father mentioned previously, is my grandfather, and the disfigured daughter is my mother. Both of them were sitting on the edge of a bed, watching over my granddaughter as she played in her crib. Both were watching from the other side of the veil, both were dressed in white, both seemed to be smiling at the happy baby. As an observer watching from a distance, everything seemed to be in perfect harmony. That is until my grandfather looked in his daughter's direction and began to weep. In an instant, I could see the regret on his face. I could feel the pain of his sorrow. I understood the depths of his grief. Here was the spirit of a man who recognized the monster he had become in mortality, and he remembered what he had done to his little girl. Seeing his grief was too much. I wanted the dream to end. But then a beautiful, sacred miracle occurred. He looked at his daughter and with sorrow filled words, he simply cried, "I'm so sorry for all I've done. Please, forgive me". Even though she had silently forgiven him already in mortality, he needed to seek her forgiveness. He needed to say the words. He needed to be released from the pain that he had carried beyond the veil. He needed to hear that she had forgiven him. In that moment, the pain and grief were gone, and love and forgiveness filled both their hearts.

I realized that since my mother is still living, my grandfather's spirit is currently weighed down with guilt as he waits for the precious opportunity to seek that forgiveness from his daughter. It hurts my heart for him. Yet at the same time, it also brings me joy to know that when my mother leaves this life, she will find him waiting for her on the other side, and she will finally have the peace that she not only deserves, but that she's longed for her entire life.

I knew at that very moment that I could not carry my secret any longer. Whether my admission of guilt happened here in mortality or on the other side of the veil, I knew it would happen. The longer I waited, the harder it would be for myself and for my loved one. I had to confront my fear and my guilt and seek forgiveness from someone who didn't even know I had betrayed them. And so I did. Instantly, like in my dream, the sorrow my grandfather felt as he sought that forgiveness, was felt in my heart as well. And grace and mercy followed shortly thereafter. Through the forgiveness I was lovingly granted, I now had to face the task of forgiving myself. This was an even greater struggle that I was not prepared for.

The gift of forgiveness and the gift of repentance are just that – gifts. They are gifts from our Heavenly Father to each of us. They are gifts of the spirit, and we need to allow those gifts to work in our lives on a daily basis. While some have the gift to forgive easily, or apologize quickly, we are all blessed with the opportunity to call upon each of these gifts when they are needed. Because each of us is ultimately a "natural man", we too are an "enemy to God" (Book of Mormon, Mosiah 3:19), and as such, we are destined to fail in mortality. We will lie, cheat, steal, gossip, bully, mock, degrade, the list goes on and on. It is because of who we are that we need these gifts, and it is because of God's love that they have been given to us.

49

In Luke chapter 15, we learn about a young man who wants to see the world and enjoy worldly pursuits. He approaches his father and asks for his inheritance that will ultimately fund his adventures. I can only assume that the father was heartbroken over his beloved son's choices, but understanding agency, the father lovingly gives his son what he asked for. The son "took his journey into a far country, and there wasted his substance with riotous living" (New Testament, Luke 15:13). There came a famine and the son had nothing left. No food to eat. No place to live. He, who once knew love and acceptance and wealth, found himself beneath that of the swine, begging for the scraps that the pigs left behind. This young man, who had nothing left, not even his pride, remembered who he was when he said unto himself, "I will arise and go to my father, and will say unto him, Father I have sinned against heaven, and before thee, and am no more worthy to be called they son; make me as one of thy hired servants" (v. 18-19). The prodigal son returned home to his father with hope that he would, at the very least, be accepted as a lowly servant. "But when he was yet a great way off, his father saw him and had compassion and ran, and fell on his neck, and kissed him" (v. 20). The young man had simply sought forgiveness and not only was it granted immediately, but all he had walked away from had been restored. The prodigal son found peace by following through on his gift of humility; he experienced happiness by seeking the gift of love from his father; he found salvation by calling upon the gift of forgiveness.

Contrast the prodigal son with the parable of the unmerciful servant found in Matthew chapter 18. In this story, the king was taking an account of what his servants had owed him. "And when he began to reckon, one was brought unto him, which owed him ten thousand talents (a very large sum of money)" (Matt. 18:24). The king then threatened to sell him, his wife, his children, and all he owned as recompense for what was owed. "The servant therefore fell down, and worshipped him, saying Lord, have patience with me, and I will pay thee all. Then the lord of the servant was moved with compassion, and loosed him, and forgave him the debt" (v.

26-27). Let us stop here for a moment. First off, notice that the servant did not willingly seek forgiveness. Instead, he had to be summoned and was then forced to answer for his debt. Only after being threatened with the loss of all he had did he seek forgiveness, which is the second point that should be made: his seeking forgiveness was not genuine.

The story continues in that after his debts were forgiven, he then went out and sought those that owed him. He found a fellow servant who was in his debt by a hundred pence, which is quite a meager amount, especially when compared to the ten thousand talents he owed the king. Instead of showing mercy as the king had shown him, he "laid hands on him, and took him by the throat, saying, Pay me what thou owest" (v. 28). The fellow servant did just as the servant did with the king and said "have patience with me, and I will pay thee all" (v. 29). The unmerciful servant still cast him into prison. In the end, the king found out about the servant having no compassion and in turn "delivered him to the tormentors, till he should pay all that was due unto him" (v. 34).

The story of the prodigal son and the parable of the unmerciful servant are quite different in their endings, but both teach the importance of forgiveness. At some point in our lives, each of us will play the part of the characters in both stories. The question we need to ask ourselves is who will we be when we stand to face our Savior? Will we be the prodigal son, and willingly seek the forgiveness we need? Will we be the servant, forced out of desperation, to plead for salvation when our hearts are not in it? Will we be the father that runs to the prodigal son and lovingly wraps him in a warm embrace? Will we be the unmerciful servant, unwilling to grant forgiveness to another?

And what of forgiving oneself? How willing are we to let go of our own past sins while working through the process of repentance? We are not defined by our sins, regardless of what the adversary wants us to think. Satan will tempt us to judge ourselves more harshly than we would a loved one, friend, or even a stranger. But I will repeat the previous words of the Savior as a stark reminder when He said, "I, the Lord, will forgive whom I will forgive, but of you it is required to forgive *all* men" (Doctrine and Covenants 64:10). It does not say you are required to forgive everyone *but* yourself; it says you are to forgive everyone *including* yourself. Do not become so discouraged with your imperfections, shortcomings, and sins, that you forget who you are. President Boyd K Packer wisely stated that "Preoccupation with unworthy behavior can lead to unworthy behavior." Let it go. If you have walked the repentant path, and you've done all you can do, then let the atonement work and do not hold yourself accountable for something that the Lord has already forgotten. Those who refuse to forgive themselves, are in fact committing an additional sin, "for there remaineth in him the greater sin" (Doctrine and Covenants 64:9).

The gift of the atonement. The gift of repentance. The gift of forgiveness. Each one of these sacred gifts was given to you and to me. They were given to the saint and the sinner. The victim and the attacker. The faithful and the disobedient. The father and the prodigal son. The master and the servant. The German prisoner and the guard. The daughter and the abusive father. The widow and the drunk driver. To you and to me.

If we cannot seek the forgiveness of another, if we cannot forgive those that hurt us, if we cannot forgive ourselves, then marriages will fail, siblings will stop speaking to each other, parents will not have a relationship with their children, friendships will die, wards will struggle, and the hearts of men will fail them. Some situations will need to be addressed with church leadership, which may make things feel more burdensome, but seek that guidance and council, and you will feel God's mercy wipe away the tears that stain your cheeks. Let us never forget the beautiful words that President Packer further taught when he lovingly reminded us that:

Save for the exception of the very few who defect to perdition, there is no habit, no addiction, no rebellion, no transgression, no apostasy, no crime exempted from the promise of complete forgiveness. That is the promise of the Atonement of Christ Do not give up if at first you fail Do not give up. That brilliant morning will come. (President Boyd K. Packer, "The Brilliant Morning of Forgiveness," Ensign, Nov. 1995)

Each of us was given gifts of the spirit and those gifts differ from person to person, but these gifts are free to all who seek them. May we strive to be worthy of the gifts of forgiveness and repentance, and live life according to the lyrics of the very wise Veggie Tales cast that sing "The Forgiveness Song" which states:

You know that in love we can forgive
It is the only way to live
Obey God and see that we can live in harmony!
Since God has forgiven us, it's true
You forgive me, I'll forgive you
I'm gonna start to show forgiveness from my heart!
You know that in love we can forgive
Hey man! It is the only way to live
Obey God and see that we can live in harmony!
Since God has forgiven us, it's true
You forgive me, I'll forgive you
I'm gonna start to show forgiveness from my heart!
So do your part and show forgiveness from your heart!

"The Forgiveness Song"; Capitol Christian Music Group Capitol CMG Publishing, 1995

Chapter 6

"Tell Her"

One of my favorite parables that the Savior taught to His disciples was that of the talents found in the New Testament in Matthew chapter 25. In short, the Savior told of a man who was preparing to leave on a long trip. He called his servants together and gave them his goods, or talents. To one he gave five talents, to another two, and to another one. To each man he gave according to his ability. While the master was away, the one that received five talents put them to good use and earned five more talents. The one that received two talents put them to use and made two more. But the servant that received the one talent buried it in the ground. Instead of using what he'd been freely given to make or earn more talents, he wasted the opportunity to increase his blessing and better his situation.

After a period of time, the master returned and asked the servants for an accounting of the talents he had given them. To the servants that had doubled their talents the master said, "Well done, good and faithful servant; thou hast been faithful over a few things, I will make thee ruler over many things: enter thou into the joy of thy lord" (Matthew 25:23). When the master had heard that the third individual hid his talent and did not multiply it, the master called him a slothful servant and said he would take the one talent from him and give it to the servant that had ten talents.

Even though the man with only one talent had less opportunities than the one with five, there was still an expectation to use and to multiply what he had received. Sadly, the servant failed himself and his master by hiding the blessing and ignoring his responsibility to use it to better his situation. Good use of the one talent was just as important and necessary as the others who were given more.

Like the servants given different talents, we too are given different gifts and talents, and we too have the same expectations to better ourselves by using our talents for good, "For the benefit of the church of the living God, that every man may improve upon his talents, that every man may gain other talents, yea, even an hundred fold" (Doctrine and Covenants 82:18). We are also reminded of the consequences of not using our talents when God says, "But with some I am not well pleased, for they will not open their mouths, but they hide the talent which I have given unto them because of the fear of men. Wo unto such, for mine anger is kindled against them. And it shall come to pass, if they are not more faithful unto me, it shall be taken away, even that which they have" (Doctrine and Covenants 60:2-3).

Up until last year, my gift was just that...mine. It was for me to use for myself. Through my visions and dreams, I learned invaluable lessons, received answers to prayers, and I'd been given guidance throughout my life, all from my Father in Heaven. Because I had never been given the opportunity to bless the lives of others, the scripture verses previously mentioned didn't carry much weight when it came to my sacred gift. Until the day that it did.

In my dream, I was calling to speak with my friend Elenore, whom I had known for several years, when her husband Rick picked up the phone and said hello. When he answered, I distinctly remember being very confused because he had unexpectedly passed away a few years prior. How, and more importantly, why was I having a conversation with someone on the other side of the veil? He seemed all too excited to chat and proceeded to tell me how great things were going, that he was in a wonderful place and was very happy, especially since all his puppies were with him. Even though I still had some confusion over this very strange phone call, I remember smiling to myself in my dream, being filled with the sweetest joy on behalf of Rick, knowing that not only was he truly happy, but he was also surrounded by his four-legged fur-babies from years past. What a delightful reunion that must have been for him. That's where the dream ended.

I woke up just as confused as I had been in my dream. Again, this gentleman had passed away a few years previous, and I hadn't talked to him for several months prior to that. Why did he show up in my dream and why did I have what seemed like a very strange conversation with him?

The dream came to me on a Sunday. As I was getting ready for church, all I could think about was that phone call in my dream, and what his lovely wife would say if I told her about it. Would she think I was a freak? Would telling her break her heart once again because it would be a stark reminder that she lost the love of her life? Would she be angry that I had the dream, and she had not? So many concerns ran through my head that entire morning. I had no idea what I was supposed to do with the information I'd been given and simply prayed that I would somehow, some way, receive an answer to the many questions rolling around in my head.

During our drive to church, my husband and I talked about the entire situation. He was a little more apprehensive about me telling her, simply because very few people knew about my gift, and he didn't want anyone to misjudge me or my intentions. Thankfully, my answer came loud and clear while I was sitting in prayerful contemplation as the sacrament was being passed. God simply said, "Tell her."

On the way home from church, my only thoughts were how and why. How was I going to start this conversation? Moreover, why, of all people, was I the one to have that dream? I practiced my speech to Elenore for several hours, and every time I went to pick up the phone, I chickened out. I couldn't do it. I was terrified to share a gift that was so sacred and so personal to me that I started fearing man over God. Towards the end of the night, I'm quite certain that God became impatient with me and just took over because the next thing I knew, I was dialing her number. She picked up on the second ring. Dang it. I momentarily cringed because there was no going back now.

She must have thought it was strange to receive a call from me out of the blue because she and I hadn't talked for several months. We got the niceties out of the way and then the butterflies hit. I began by simply stating, "This conversation is going to sound very bizarre, but I have been strongly prompted to call and tell you about an experience I had recently, and I hope and pray that you don't think I'm crazy." She laughed and simply said OK.

I then spent the next several minutes explaining my gift as she sat and listened attentively. Then, with a brief and hesitant sigh, I launched into the story of my dream. After I finished detailing what I had experienced, I paused to catch my breath. I tried so hard not to ramble and rush through it, but the amount of adrenaline inside my heart made it nearly impossible to stay calm. I waited through what seemed like an eternal silence until she finally responded with, "Wow." I wondered at first if it was a good wow or a bad wow. She paused once again, and I was convinced her hesitation meant that she was never going to want to speak to me again. Our friendship was doomed. She would believe that I was utterly crazy and truly a freak. To my utter relief, the tenderest of mercies happened just then.

This beautiful, humble friend of mine, who had endured so much sadness, thanked me for answering her prayers. She stated that she had been missing her beloved husband more than usual over the previous few months and had been praying for a sign that he was happy. She had been pleading with God to hear from him just one more time. She then proceeded to tell me that she knew, without a doubt, that her husband had come to me in a dream because he had mentioned that his puppies were with him. He had dogs around him his entire life and loved each one of them fiercely. That was information I hadn't known until that very moment.

We chatted for a while longer until she circled back around to my dream. Thanking me profusely for having the courage to call, she stated she would never forget that I was the vehicle in which God had answered her prayers. I remember being slightly uncomfortable wondering why me. There were so many other avenues that God could have used to bless her with the answers she desperately needed. Why had He chosen me? After voicing my uneasiness, she simply said, "Because my husband loved your family, and God knew you wouldn't keep that information to yourself. He knew you would do the right thing."

Even now, I shake my head in wonder at the miraculous hand of God, the amount of love He had for my dear friend to answer such a humble prayer, and the amount of trust He had in me to follow through. All of these realizations came because of my gift and the fact that I did not let fear stop me from sharing it to bless the life of another; I did not bury my talent in the ground as the servant had.

The scriptures are full of examples where others were blessed because of the actions of one person. Prophets, apostles, and various messengers are constantly helping and giving to others in the scriptures. But what about the everyday messengers and angels that God sends to each of us. Are we paying attention to that still small voice that says, "Reach out, and do not fear"? Are we using our gifts to bless those in need that God places in our path? Are we putting our talents to good use and allowing them to multiply whenever possible?

Initially, when I started thinking about this very idea, I assumed that I would only be able to think of a few examples, but once I started, the flood gates opened. I've seen a sister who has worked with the youth for many years in different capacities, whose gift is being able to connect with teenagers (truly a miracle indeed). She is able to reach troubled teens and help them stay focused on the right path when most others would have given up on them. I've seen a sister build a social media presence to help others with food storage, cooking and baking, getting out of debt, and generally being more prepared in these latter days because she was blessed with the gift of preparedness and homemaking. I like to think of her as a cross between a modern-day Betty Crocker and a sassy June Cleaver with apocalyptic survival skills that she shares with anyone and everyone she meets. I knew a gentleman whose gift was understanding law and as a result, he became a very successful attorney. He used his gift to write up contracts for couples wading through the adoption process, and he offered his gift free of charge. Lastly, if you don't know Al Fox Caraway, also known as the 'tattooed Mormon', then you truly are missing out. She is an amazing example of someone who uses her gift of public speaking, teaching, and writing, to bring others unto Christ.

Several years ago, my husband had major back surgery due to an incident with one of our horses. He was in constant pain all day, every day, and was struggling physically and mentally because of his sudden lack of mobility. It was during this time that our ward boundaries changed due to the growth of the church in our area. As a result, we were one of the few families that were assigned to a new ward in a completely different building. Needless to say, our family was sad that we would no longer see our friends every Sunday, but we knew that God's handiwork was in motion.

On our second Sunday in the new ward, my husband was having a particularly difficult time with his back and ended up standing in the foyer for most of Sacrament meeting, Sunday School, and Priesthood simply because of how painful it was to sit down. As we were leaving, a gentleman approached him and asked how he was. My husband explained his situation, and his new friend responded that he was a chiropractor and, if given the opportunity, he would be able to help alleviate the pain in my husband's back. Due to a previously bad

59

experience with chiropractic work, my husband was apprehensive to say the least, but after a few more weeks of misery, he finally conceded and went to see this doctor at his office. It only took a few visits before my husband got his life back, and it only took a few more weeks before those two boys became the best of friends. And none of it would have happened if God had not intervened with the changing of the ward boundaries, or if Dr. Smith had not listened to the promptings he received and used his gift of healing to approach and offer to help a brother in need.

I never imagined that I would be given the opportunity to bless the lives of others because of my dreams, but God, in His wisdom, taught me otherwise. What I learned through this experience is that we all have gifts that seem to only benefit ourselves, but if we are in tune with the Spirit, and we sincerely seek to understand and use our gifts, we will be given an opportunity to multiply our talents. However, like the servants in the parable, it is up to us to either use our gifts or bury them when those opportunities present themselves. Elder Robert D. Hales advised us that "As we follow [the Savior], He blesses us with gifts, talents, and the strength to do His will, allowing us to go beyond our comfort zones and do things we've never before thought possible" ('Being a More Christian Christian'; General Conference, Oct. 2012).

Some gifts are obvious when it comes to having the ability to bless others. If you sing or play an instrument, using those gifts to share the gospel, provide teaching opportunities for less fortunate individuals, or perform for an audience is a given. If you have the gift of making friends, then fulfilling your calling as a ministering brother or sister should come easily. Has your gift allowed you to become an English major? Write a gospel centered children's book or teach an English class to those who speak a different language. What if you're an artist. You could create a beautiful depiction of the eternal love between a husband and wife. A photographer? Take pictures of temples and give them to the primary children. There are endless ways we can use our gifts to bless the lives of others, but what about the more inconspicuous gifts, or those that may sometimes feel like a burden?

I recently met a missionary who openly discussed the struggles he faces everyday as a result of having Autism Spectrum Disorder. He admitted that when he was considering a mission, he initially hoped he would be called to a service mission, unsure of how successful he would be as a proselytizing missionary. Regardless, he trusted in God's plan and had faith that he would be called to serve wherever he was needed. He submitted his papers and waited. To his complete surprise, he was called to serve as a proselytizing missionary in Tennessee. He admitted that he was apprehensive at first but trusted in the path he was asked to walk. He also knew that his gifts were that of clear knowledge and personal confidence. Furthermore, he began to understand that although his autism was a struggle, it was less of a disorder and more of a gift as well. His gift of knowledge allowed him to remember the lessons he'd been taught in his youth and easily retain what he learned in his studies, and as a result it gave him the gift of confidence to boldly teach the gospel and to be a tool in the Lord's hands. He used his gifts to bless the lives of others through his obedience to serve a teaching mission, even though it made the path he was asked to walk a little more difficult.

If we apply the parable of the talents to our own lives, then we are forced to take an inventory of the gifts that we have been given. As I said previously, I never truly appreciated this lesson until it applied to my own life. I was not using my gift to bless the lives of others simply because I didn't know how. I had not taken the time to study, ponder, and pray. I had assumed that Heavenly Father would guide my life whenever I needed it. I selfishly kept my gift to myself, but once I understood how I could use it to bless the lives of others, I went to my Father and sincerely prayed to have guidance and then He helped me write this book.

Each of us will have at least one gift that may seem of little use to anyone but ourselves, but I promise that if you ponder on each of your gifts, especially the ones that only seem to benefit you, and then sincerely pray to know how to use those gifts to bless the lives of others, I can assure you that your eyes will be opened to limitless possibilities. Let us all be wise like the servants who multiplied their talents so we can be blessed with an abundance so rich that we cannot number all we have. And may we strive to live worthy of hearing the sweet words of our Lord who will certainly say "Well done, thou good and faithful servant." And may we live our lives according to the simply perfect words of Hillary Weeks in her song titled, "Not Too Far From Here".

Somebody's down to their last dime

Somebody's running out of time

Not too far from here

Somebody's got nowhere else to go

Somebody needs a little hope

Not too far from here

Somebody's troubled and confused

Somebody's got nothin' left to lose

Not too far from here

Somebody's forgotten how to trust

Somebody's dyin' for love

Not too far from here

And I may not know their name

But I'm praying just the same

That You'll use me, Lord

To wipe away the tears

'Cause somebody's crying

Not too far from here

Songwriters: Steve Siler / Ty Lacy
"Not Too Far From Here"; Capitol Christian Music Group, Capitol CMG
Publishing, Sony/ATV Music Publishing LLC, 2007

Chapter 7

'Why?'

According to the National Institute of Mental Health Disorders, an estimated 26% of Americans ages 18 and older, about 1 in 4 adults, will suffer from a diagnosable mental disorder in a given year. Some will experience one disorder, and some will have the struggle of many. For some, it will be genetic; for others, environmental. Some may have to battle clinical disorders that last several years and possibly even throughout one's lifetime, and others like myself, will experience situational disorders that occur as the result of a trauma, or a significant life changing event. Regardless of our individual struggles, whether mental, physical, emotional, or spiritual, it is imperative that we always remember that we are not alone. In any situation. Ever.

We are reminded in the Book of Mormon in Alma, Chapter 7 that "[the Savior] shall go forth, suffering pains and afflictions and temptations of *every kind*" And because of his sacrificial act of absolute love for both you and me, he understands all our pains and afflictions and temptations of *every kind*. He knows exactly how we feel. He knows our struggles. He knows our frustrations. He knows our weaknesses. And He knows what it feels like to be without the comfort of the Holy Ghost. He knows because He was the one that "cried with a loud voice, saying...My God, my God, why hast thou forsaken me (New Testament, Mark 15:34)?"

I cannot not comprehend, nor will I ever know the depths to which my Savior went to atone for my heartaches of the past, and the ones which I have yet to experience. For He truly felt all the fear, the anxiety, the depression, the helplessness, the anger, and the darkness. He suffered the feelings of abandonment. Because of that, we do not have to climb our mountainous trials or carry our burdensome crosses alone. However, that does not make our journey less difficult.

My childhood and young adult years were riddled with different levels and degrees of trauma that included physical, emotional, and sexual abuse, as well as addiction and all the adverse effects of watching someone you love become a slave to their dependence. But even through it all, I stayed strong, focused my attention on not becoming an addiction statistic, and did my best to claw my way out of generational abuse.

During that time, I maintained excellent grades in school, tried to stay out of trouble as much as possible, and didn't let my home life affect my own drive to do and be better. For the most part, I succeeded in dealing with all that trauma on my own. That is until 35 years later when, in one singular traumatizing moment, my tightly controlled, compartmentalized box exploded into a million tiny pieces, exposing years of suppressed torment, and my whole world came crashing down in the blink of an eye.

This one moment in time made me question everything, and everyone, including my Savior. I could not get a grip on my emotions, and it felt like I was drowning into the depths of the sea. The more I fought to get to the surface for air, the further down I sank. I was desperately trying to hold on to my sanity while it slowly slipped right through my fingers. After several weeks, my husband lovingly suggested that I seek the help of a professional, and I willingly agreed. After a few sessions, my therapist advised that I would benefit from a type of therapy called EMDR, or Eye Movement Desensitization and Reprocessing. EMDR is a form of psychotherapy which requires a person to recall, in vivid detail, the trauma that was experienced, while the therapist directs the patient in a repetitive eye movement. This process allows for the memory, or the trauma, to be 'dislodged' and processed in a way that allows the brain to recover and heal from said trauma. EMDR therapy is hard. It is emotionally taxing beyond anything I had yet to experience, aside from the trauma itself, because I had to go back to the very moment that caused the trauma in the first place. And I had multiple traumas to deal with.

One evening, after a particularly difficult therapy session, I was an emotional wreck. I was sitting up in bed trying to describe to my very patient husband all that I was feeling, and everything that was discussed with my therapist, but the tears would not stop falling. I was running out of tissues and breathing through my nose became impossible. I was nauseated and doing the crying hiccup. In short, I had a full-blown meltdown. And all I kept saying, over and over again, was 'Why?' 'Why did all those bad things happen?' 'Why does it have to be so hard now?' 'Why can't I just get past all this?' Those were the questions that I kept asking my husband, who was at a complete loss on how to respond. Why did it have to be so hard? After I finally settled down, and things were dark and quiet outside, and the thoughts in my head had calmed, my sweet husband offered to give me a Priesthood blessing. Such an obvious thing to suggest, but one that had never crossed my mind while I anguished in the utter depths of my despair.

Hands were placed on my head, the Melchizedek Priesthood was called upon, and the blessing began. As the words were spoken, a very clear vision played like a movie in my head. "Heavenly Father needs you to know that it had to be so hard because once you are on the other side of the veil, you will have spirit children sitting at your feet, learning from your mortal experiences. You will need to teach them how to survive in a hardened world, so that they too can return to live with Him again." In that moment, I was dressed in white, with many children sitting at my feet, listening attentively and learning what I had to teach them. And my beautiful Isabella, my sweet little girl who I searched for relentlessly in a dream years previous, was there, dressed in white, just as before. And in that moment, I understood the truest definition of what it means to keep an eternal perspective. Heavenly Father had used my gift to calm my fears; He used my gift to answer my prayers; He used my gift to give me insight into the whys of my struggles.

In December 1838, the prophet Joseph Smith, and a few of his companions, were arrested and unjustly held in Liberty Jail until April 1839, a span of 4 months. During their confinement, these men were forced to sleep on dirty straw scattered on hard floors and were fed spoiled and rotted food. The jail was so confining that Joseph couldn't stand to his full height, and because it was the middle of winter, they were left to deal with the harshness of the cold without the warmth of winter clothes or blankets. Their situation was dire indeed.

Not only were Joseph and his friends in miserable conditions, but they also had to bear the burden of knowing their families were being persecuted and driven from their homes, and there was nothing these men could do to help. It was during a moment of total despair that Joseph cried out, "O God, where are thou? And where is the pavilion that covereth thy hiding place" (Doctrine and Covenants 121:1)? Joseph was feeling abandoned, and alone. A feeling that we have all faced at some point in our lives. And like Joseph, we too have cried out to God, pleading for Him to come to our aide, or we've begged to know why our trials had to be so hard.

Joseph continued his plea with, "How long shall thy hand be stayed?" "How long shall they [the saints] suffer these wrongs and unlawful oppressions, before thine heart shall be softened toward them" (Doctrine and Covenants 121:2-3)? God's reply was simple. "My son, peace be unto thy soul; thine adversity and thine afflictions shall be but a small moment; And then, if thou endure it well, God shall exalt thee on high; thou shalt triumph over all thy foes" (Doctrine and Covenants 121:7-8). God continued His loving, yet honest reply, giving Joseph the perspective that he needed, with these words:

And if thou shouldst be cast into the pit, or into the hands of murders, and the sentence of death passed before thee; if thou be cast into the deep; if the billowing surge conspire against thee; if fierce winds become thine enemy; if the heavens gather blackness, and all the elements combine to hedge up the way; and above all if the very jaws of hell shall gape open the mouth wide after thee, know thou, my son, that all these things shall give thee experience, and shall be for thy good. The Son of Man hath descended below them all. Art thou greater than he? (Doctrine and Covenants 122:7-8)

It was during one of the prophet's darkest hours that the Lord gave him an eternal perspective. He reminded Joseph that patiently enduring trials, burdens, heartaches, and all things hard, is required as part of our mortal experience. It allows us to strengthen our testimonies, which draws us closer to our Heavenly Father, and will eventually result in gaining the exaltation that for now, is only a longing hope.

Joseph's living conditions had not improved after he received God's reply. He was still in a miserable situation, but his understanding had significantly increased. His mindset had changed for the better, and it didn't take long before he once again became the leader that the saints so willingly followed. Shortly after his answers came, the prophet addressed his growing flock, urging them not to lose hope when he said, "let us cheerfully do all things that lie in our power; and then may we stand still, with the utmost assurance, to see the salvation of God, and for his arm to be revealed" (Doctrine and Covenants 123:17).

I imagine Joseph Smith had many gifts of the spirit, but his ability to gain additional knowledge on what keeping an eternal perspective means, started with his gift of prayer, a gift that he chose to call upon in a moment of severe frustration and self-doubt, a moment that ended up being a turning point in how he viewed his trials. And like Joseph, we too can be blessed with a deeper understanding of the eternities if we allow Heavenly Father to use our gifts to open our eyes to the possibilities that await us on the other side of the veil. Elder Dallin H. Oaks reminded us of this very important doctrine when he stated, "Seen with the perspective of eternity, a temporal setback can be an opportunity to develop soul power of eternal significance. Strength is forged in adversity. Faith is developed in a setting where we cannot see what lies ahead" (Dallin H. Oaks, 'Spirituality', General Conference, October 1985).

The difficult part about gaining a stronger testimony on keeping an eternal perspective is that we must first endure the trial. It was Peter that said,

The trial of your faith, being much more precious than of gold that perisheth, though it be tried with fire, might be found unto praise and honour and glory at the appearing of Jesus Christ: Whom having not seen, ye love; in whom, though now ye see him not, yet believing, ye rejoice with joy unspeakable and full of glory: Receiving the end of your faith even the salvation of your souls (New Testament, 1 Peter 1:7-9).

Did you catch what Peter said? It's not our faith that matters most, but the *trial of our faith* that's more precious than gold. It is not the trial itself, but rather our perspective and the choices we make as we endure them. Elder Neil L. Anderson said it best when he stated:

These fiery trials are designed to make you stronger, but they have the potential to diminish or even destroy your trust in the Son of God and to weaken your resolve to keep your promises to Him They take root in our weaknesses, our vulnerabilities, our sensitivities, or in those things that matter most to us[But] how do you remain steadfast and immovable during a trial of your faith? You immerse yourself in the very things that helped build your core of faith: you exercise faith in Christ, you pray, you ponder the scriptures, you repent, you keep the commandments, and you serve others (Elder Neil L. Anderson, 'Trial of Your Faith', General Conference, October 2012).

I would also add to the above that we need to keep an eternal perspective.

One day, I was speaking with a very good friend of mine and we happen to be on the subject of spiritual gifts. I asked her what gift God had blessed her with, and without pause, she laughed and said, "I have the gift of appreciating my trials and burdens, because I know they could always be worse." She went on to explain that after her divorce, while she was struggling as a single mom and financially burdened, she was grateful that she was no longer in an abusive situation. And when her mom passed away from cancer, she certainly mourned her death, but was grateful that it wasn't her son. And most recently, while hospitalized for several weeks with Covid, having no physical contact with her family, and not knowing if she would live or die, she was grateful for the opportunity to reflect on her relationship with her Heavenly Father, reminding herself that if she was taken to the other side of the veil, at least she had a testimony of the Savior and she knew who He was. This beautiful sister found peace in the middle of an ICU room while listening to machines beep incessantly, hearing the code calls and running feet pounding on the floors as the medical staff ran to save a patient, and felt the sadness when one was called home from this life. She found peace, while staring death in the face, because she used her gift of knowing things could be worse and God blessed her with a deeper understanding of how important it was to keep an eternal perspective.

Each of us will have different gifts. It may not be obvious on how to use those gifts to keep an eternal perspective, or how to allow God to show us that perspective when we need it, but thoughtful prayer and contemplation will get you the answers you seek. An eternal perspective can be seen in our children's faces for those blessed with the gift of parenthood. Maybe your gift is that of financial independence, and through a trial or misfortune, you are reminded that money cannot buy your salvation, and God gives you better insight on how to use those finances to bless the lives of others. If you have the gift of motivation, you may find yourself struggling with a weakness that is frustrating and discouraging. Maintaining that motivation when things are hard may require a lot more humility in asking for God's help, but the meek shall inherit the earth. Perhaps your trial involves learning disabilities and you find it difficult to remember what you read. You may find yourself in the midst of a trial and after many prayers for mercy, your answer may be to read the scriptures, which may seem quite frustrating, given your struggles. But then God gives you an eternal perspective when He reminds you that our minds and bodies will be whole again, and even if retrieving information from your memories now may seem impossible, all that we learn in this life will be readily available to us in the eternities.

Not only can and should we use our gifts to keep an eternal perspective, but they will also help to keep us humble, and may cause us to stumble in such a way that we wish our gift wasn't a gift at all. This particular lesson on humility took me a little longer to learn than I care to admit. My Patriarchal Blessing states that I have the gift of being an example to my family and friends, with the promise that they will someday return to the gospel and chose to live righteous lives once again. I have held tight to that promise but didn't quite understand the full meaning of my responsibility until my PTSD (Post Traumatic Stress Disorder) and anxiety gut punched me from out of the blue. It literally brought me to my knees.

If given the choice, I would have preferred setting the example by continuing to do the things I had been doing, like attending church, fulfilling my calling, reading my scriptures, and saying My prayers, but what good would it do me if I didn't have similar struggles to those I love most? How could I ever encourage or inspire my friends and family

71

without first going through trials that are comparable? I could easily empathize with them, but in order for me to show others the way, I would need to lead by example and overcome similar challenges.

My gift, and calling, is to show my family and friends how to emerge from the depths of despair, but I must experience that despair myself to truly lead the way. If your calling is to mend broken hearts, then you will most assuredly experience a broken heartedness that may leave you thinking your spirit will never mend. Maybe your gift is that of empowerment, but you wonder why you often have bouts of uncertainty so extreme that your own foundation is shaken to its core. Or you have the gift of obedience, but you find yourself struggling to follow the Prophet on a particular church policy and sustaining him becomes increasingly more difficult. Your gift will come with burdens, crosses, sifting and thorns, all of which are necessary for your eternal perspective to be genuine, inspiring, and powerful. Your gifts may not be easy, because your calling will not be easy, and truly understanding an eternal perspective will require "an opposition in all things" (Book of Mormon, 2Nephi 2:11). We must always remember that the foundation of our gift can only be strengthened by enduring life's fiery darts and that keeping an eternal perspective will shield us from those very darts that the adversary will throw our way. If we can trust that Heavenly Father's eternal plan will always be for our good, then one day, we will have the opportunity to look back and thank Him for those very same experiences that gave us a perspective that we would not have gained in any other fashion.

Regardless of the trials you face, or the weaknesses you struggle with, God can and will use your gifts to help strengthen your confidence and help you remember that you have divine potential. For it is only after enduring our most difficult adversities that we will be blessed with further enlightenment, allowing us to draw closer to the Savior, and continue working out our salvation. Let us all be like Elder Joseph B. Wirthlin's beloved mother who said, "Come what may, and love it" (Elder Joseph B.

Wirthlin, 'Come What May, and Love It', General Conference, October 2008).

I once read a story called "The Biscuits, The Farmer, and an Amen", that at first made me laugh, until the very end, when I realized the truth within the story. May we strive to remember to keep an eternal perspective when things are not going as smoothly as we'd like. And let us always be patient during the mixin' so that we may enjoy the eternities, which will always be better than the biscuits.

There once was a new pastor attending a men's breakfast in a rural area.

He asked one of the old farmers in attendance to offer the prayer on the food.

After all were seated, the old farmer began:

"Lord, I hate buttermilk."

The pastor opened one eye and wondered where this was going.

Then the farmer loudly proclaimed, "Lord, I hate lard."

At this point, the pastor began to worry, however without missing a beat, the farmer prayed on.

"And Lord, you know I don't care much for raw white flour."

Just as the Pastor was about to stand up and stop the prayer, the farmer concluded with:

"But Lord, when You mix'em all together and bake'em up, I do love fresh biscuits.

So Lord, when things come up that we don't like, when life gets hard, when we just don't understand what You're a sayin' to us, please bless us so we can wait 'til you're done mixin'.

And probably Lord, it will be somethin' even better than biscuits.

Amen."

(Arthur Unknown)

Chapter 8

'I Choose God'

"Latter-day Saints know that there is a God. With like certainty, they know that Satan lives, that he is a powerful personage of spirit, the archenemy of God, of man, and of righteousness" (President Marion G. Romney, 'Satan, The Great Deceiver', General Conference, April 1971). The reality of these words spoken by President Romney hold an absolute truth that we must never forget: Satan lives. One of the most foolish things we can do as individuals and Christians is to deny the existence of his evil power, his influence, and his unending fight against all that is good. He knows our strengths, our talents and our gifts, just as the Savior does. He knows our fears, our weaknesses and our blind spots, just as the Savior does. Satan knows us individually, just as the Savior does. And if we are not consciously choosing to follow Jesus Christ, then we are unconsciously choosing to follow the adversary. And it is guaranteed that he will slowly lead us down a path of total destruction, especially if we are allowing the distractions of life to get in the way, causing us to miss the warning signs of truth.

Satan is the father of lies and deceit. He is a skillful imitator of gospel truths and is no respecter of persons. He descended upon Joseph Smith in the Sacred Grove, just prior to the First Vision, and in Joseph's own words, he "had such an astonishing influence over me as to bind my tongue so that I could not speak. Thick darkness gathered around me, and it seemed to me for a time as if I were doomed to sudden destruction" (Joseph Smith History 1:15). In the Book of Mormon, He blinded Alma the younger against all that his father, Alma Sr, had taught among the people of Mosiah, so much so that Alma the Younger became a very wicked man. Alma "led many of the people to do after the manner of his iniquities he became a great hinderment of the prosperity of the church of God;

stealing away the hearts of the people; causing much dissension" (Mosiah 27:7-8).

There are several more examples of the cunning work of the adversary including Laman and Lemuel in the Book of Mormon, and the hardening of their hearts. Judas Iscariot when he betrayed Jesus in the New Testament, who was his friend and mentor. Adam and Eve when he tempted them with the fruit of the tree of knowledge of good and evil in the Old Testament. And even our Jesus, the Jehovah of the Old Testament, the Messiah of the New Testament, the Savior of all mankind.

The prince of darkness is not foolish. He is quite cunning and knows when to strike; he knows when we are at our lowest and conveniently takes advantage of the situation when he feels we are powerless to his allurements. In the New Testament in Matthew, chapter 4, we learn that Jesus traveled into the wilderness to be with His Father, and after fasting forty days and forty nights, He found himself in a weakened state, both mentally and physically. It was in this moment of vulnerability that the devil presented tests for the Savior to prove himself to be the Son of God. He knew Christ had fasted and was hungry, so he tempted him with turning stones into bread for nourishment. Jesus responded with, "It is written, Man shall not live by bread alone, but by every word that proceedeth out of the mouth of God" (Matthew 4:4). Satan knew that Jesus had the power to save others so he lifted Jesus to the top of the temple and suggested that he jump off and have the angels descend and save him, for the Son of God surely would be protected from death. But Jesus simply replied, "It is written again, Thou shalt not tempt the Lord thy God" (Matthew 4:7). And lastly, after the two previous attempts failed, the masterful devil tempted Jesus with his power and all the possessions of the earth. Jesus rebuked Satan with His own power when He said, "Get thee hence, Satan: for it is written, Thou shalt worship the Lord thy God, and him only shalt thou serve" (Matthew 4:10).

It was only after the Savior endured the trials placed before him by the enemy that "the devil leaveth him, and, behold, angels came down and ministered unto him" (Matthew 4:11). Jesus was tempted but withstood the enticements of the prince of darkness. Paul taught us that this test was needed, "For in that he himself hath suffered being tempted, he is able to succour them that are tempted" (Hebrews 2:18). Satan had lost. And so it needs to be with each of us in our own personal battle against the adversary. He will tempt us, but we must endure and when we do the angels will minister unto us as well.

Heavenly Father, in all His beautiful wisdom, knew what would shortly come to pass in my life. He also knew that I would need help to fight against the cunningness of the adversary, and that I would need a focus to keep moving forward on my personal journey back to Him. As a result, I was called to be the seminary teacher. I was thoroughly confused at this turn of events because my life was a chaotic mess due to working a full-time job and taking a certification class online. Not only that, but we had recently purchased a new home and we were in the middle of a full renovation, but I accepted my new calling, nonetheless. A few short months later, I was faced with a trial unlike any I had previously endured. It was during my struggle with PTSD as mentioned in the previous chapter. My trauma struggles were a devastatingly low point in my life, so of course the adversary decided to play a cruel joke on me, because let's be honest, he's a big fat jerk.

The dream felt real. It felt as revelatory as the ones previous. It felt like God, in His mercy, was warning me. I was standing in my kitchen, dressed in a black skirt and blazer, with my hands spread out on the counter, in an attempt to keep myself composed and upright. There were several people mingling on the porch outside when the screen door opened, and a long-time family friend approached asking if I was ok. As tears started rolling down my cheeks, I simply shook my head and said, "James, I don't know how to do this. I don't know how to go on without him." It was at that moment that I realized my sweet husband, my best friend of almost thirty years, had died. I woke up in a panic with my heart racing, and very real tears now rolling down my cheeks. I reached over to ensure my husband was still there next to me, and that he was in fact breathing, and then I quietly crawled out of bed, went downstairs and sobbed. Alone.

Was God trying to prepare me for what was to come? Was He telling me to get our affairs in order? Was this a dream of mercy because Heavenly Father knew how crushing it would be for me to endure a life without my eternal companion? How would my husband die? Would it be quick and painless, or a tragic accident? So many questions, so much anxiety. And it felt so very real. As I said, the dream felt just as revelatory as the others. Throughout that day I had to remind myself, repeatedly, of the Plan of Salvation and that death will always be a part of mortality, but the harder I tried to come to terms with the possibility of losing my husband, the heavier the weight of the reality became; it was too much to bear. Later that night, I got in the shower, turned the water on as hot as I could stand, and sobbed until it felt as though my tears had outnumbered the millions of hot water drops pouring down upon my body.

It was in that moment that I remembered 2 Timothy 1:7 in the New Testament (thanks to my seminary calling) which states, "For God hath not given us the spirit of fear; but of power, and of love, and of a sound mind." And with that thought, I knew. I knew it wasn't God. I knew it wasn't a warning. It was a hellish imitation from the adversary. I was overcome with despair; not power, not love, and certainly not a sound mind. I quietly whispered over, and over again, "I choose God. I choose God. I choose God." My whispers became louder and louder until I was sure that Satan heard my fierce cries of rejection to his merciless game. And then, slowly but surely, the angels descended. Fear was replaced with comfort. Anxiety was replaced with peace. Questions were replaced with confidence as I remembered that God is not a god of fear.

And in a matter of seconds, my mind was pricked with a memory from a few years previous. My husband and I were asked to be temple workers in the Nashville, Tennessee Temple. As part of working in the temple, we were each given a blessing of guidance, and comfort. It was during my husband's blessing that he received a vision of his own. During our drive home that evening after our shift in the temple, he shared with me what he saw in a vision as he watched the scene from above. He relayed that he was an elderly gentleman, slowly shuffling his way down the hallway in the temple, with paperwork in his hand. He was the Sealer; he was the one that had the authority to marry and seal couples for time and all eternity. It was a tender mercy that his vision from a few years before became an answer to my plea for peace. My eternal companion would live a much longer life than what I had seen in my nightmarish dream. I was tempted to let fear and doubt lead me from the light of God's love, and even though it took me all day to emerge from the pit of hell that Satan had me in, I fought back, and I had won. Satan had lost the battle.

I had always known Satan was real. I had previous experiences with his temptations and the dark and ominous feelings that can only come from him. We've all been there. But it wasn't until after this incident that I began to wonder just how much power the adversary really had. And it made me more aware of when I felt the fear and doubt start to take hold of my emotions. But how was it possible for him to gain access to my gift of spiritual dreams? My answer came several months later during my study of Moses, and his initial attempts to free the children of Israel from bondage in Egypt.

In the Old Testament in Exodus, chapter 7, we see how Satan can, and does counterfeit God's power. At this point in the story, Moses and Aaron had presented themselves before Pharaoh, asking for the people to be freed. Pharaoh does not heed the warnings given, and thus begins the onset of the ten plagues.

In an effort to show Pharoah God's power, Aaron "cast down his rod before Pharaoh, and before his servants, and it became a serpent...Then Pharaoh also called the wise men and the sorcerers: now the magicians of Egypt, they also did in like manner with their enchantments. For they cast down every man his rod, and they became serpents; but Aaron's rod swallowed up their rods" (Exodus 7:10-12). Pharaoh's sorcerers were able to call upon Satan's power to do as Aaron had done and turned their rods into serpents. Next, the Lord tells Moses and Aaron to turn the waters to blood. "and he [Aaron] lifted up the rod, and smote the waters that were in the river, in the sight of Pharaoh, and in the sight of his servants; and all the waters that were in the river were turned to blood. And the magicians of Egypt did so with their enchantments" (Exodus 7:20-22). Again, the magicians were able to mimic the power God had given to Moses and Aaron.

Pharaoh's magicians continued their evil imitations in Exodus chapter 8 with the frogs in the third plague. It wasn't until the fourth plague, that of the lice, that the sorcerers were unable to copy that which was done by Moses. At this point, they even pleaded with Pharaoh to end the torment when they said "this is the finger of God; and Pharaoh's heart was hardened, and he hearkened not unto them" (Exodus 8:17-19). This example was a very clear indication to me of just how powerful Satan and his hosts are. And even though he is under the limitations placed upon him by God, he will try to mimic every power, every gift, every blessing and every gospel doctrine in his attempts to lure us to deny and reject that which is pure, and good, and true.

Satan has had the power to deceive man from the beginning of time, up to today, and will continue to do so, until he is bound. He will continue to send his evil minions throughout the world and even into our homes, but he will not prevail in our personal battles unless we allow it, and he will certainly never win the war. But in order to withstand, deny and more importantly, defeat his presence and influence, we must, "Put on the whole armour of God, that [we] may be able to stand against the wiles of the devil. For we wrestle not against flesh and blood, but against principalities, against powers, against the rulers of the darkness of this world" (New Testament, Ephesians 6:11–12).

So how do we fight against that darkness? How do we protect our gifts, ourselves and our loved ones? How do we learn to recognize the lies, the counterfeits, and the imitations? We must go back to the basics. Our first priority is to keep the Spirit with us at all times, and in all things, and in all places. And then we must work to learn and understand our gifts. Because again, Satan knows our gifts; we cannot win a battle that we are not prepared to fight. Elder Marion G Romney gave us great counsel during the when he said:

> We know that to qualify us to prevail against Satan and his wicked hosts, we have been given the gospel of Jesus Christ. We know that the Spirit of Christ and the power of his priesthood are ample shields to the power of Satan. We know that there is available to each of us the gift of the Holy Ghost—the power of revelation which embraces the gift of discernment by which we may unerringly detect the devil and the counterfeits he is so successfully foisting upon this gullible generation. Our course is clear and certain. It is to strictly obey the commandments of the Lord, as they are recorded in the scriptures and as they are being given by the living prophets ("Satan – The Great Deceiver"; General Conference, April 1971).

So how do we fight against that darkness? The answer is simple: obey the commandments and follow the prophet. Oh, and use your gifts! It took me a long time to realize that our gifts are also our greatest personal weapon against Satan and his followers, so use them.

If you have the gift of leading others, be mindful to pray for guidance that you are not 'prompted' to teach inaccurate or inappropriate material.

81

I've seen situations within the church where righteous leaders were blinded by worldly opinions that were in opposition to gospel principles, and as a result those worldly opinions began to be accepted among those in leadership roles. If you have the gift of obedience, be careful not to judge others who may struggle along the way. Regardless of this gift, there are no perfectly obedient members. And while obedience may come easier to some, Satan will tempt you into thinking you 'deserve' certain callings in the church, or positions at work, or blessings you feel are owed because of your obedience. If you have the gift of healing, do not let pride blind you to the fact that your healing powers are from God, and not just because you are 'educated and good at what you do'. If you have the gift of obeying the Word of Wisdom, never underestimate the addictiveness of legally prescribed drugs, and that diet and exercise can also become addictive and taken to the extreme. If your gift is that of knowledge, do not become complacent in continuing your education, and do not allow the adversary to confuse 'your' knowledge with that of your gift.

If you have the gift of being a parent, Satan's influence and power absolutely cannot be underestimated; he will find his way to your children. Elder Robert D Hales stated:

> Because of the importance of the family to the eternal plan of happiness, Satan makes a major effort to destroy the sanctity of the family, demean the importance of the role of men and women, encourage moral uncleanliness and violations of the sacred law of chastity, and to discourage parents from placing the bearing and rearing of children as one of their highest priorities" (Ensign: Strengthening the Family; Dec 2004).

We must protect our sacred gift of children from him who would destroy them. It is important to remember that children need boundaries and discipline, as well as being educated on the views of the world while maintaining their innocence. The gift of parenting will require constant diligence in seeking guidance and direction from Heavenly Father. Your children need to be allowed to fail at home so they will be better prepared to handle the world once they are no longer under the safety of your roof. Our children are also blessed with gifts, which the adversary knows all too well, and in order for them to withstand the onslaught of the evils of the world, parents must teach their children the gospel in every aspect of their lives, including guidance on how to use their gifts and how the adversary will use manipulation of that gift to lead them astray. We learn from Joseph Fielding Smith that:

> Spiritual solidarity in family relationships is the sure foundation upon which the Church and society itself will flourish. This fact is well known and appreciated by the adversary, and as never before, he is using every clever device, influence, and power within his control to undermine and destroy this eternal institution. Only the gospel of Jesus Christ applied in family relationships will thwart this devilish destructiveness. There are many great and real dangers to be reckoned with, and those which concern us more than all others combined have to do with our children" (The Teachings of Joseph Fielding Smith; Chapter 16, Bringing Up Children in Truth and Light).

I cannot emphasize enough the importance of learning and understanding your gifts in such a way that when the adversary cleverly sneaks in to imitate that gift, that you are spiritually prepared to quickly recognize his counterfeits and are able withstand his manipulations enough to win the battle against evil. I understood his ability to influence my mind during sleep because of night terrors that I've had over the years, but I was completely ignorant of his power to mimic a spiritual dream and was wholly unprepared to fight against it. I have since learned to promptly seek the guidance of the Holy Ghost in any situation where my gifts are concerned if there is even the slightest prick of uncertainty or doubt. It was a hard lesson to learn but one that was vital in strengthening my relationship with Heavenly Father, as well as understanding that Satan is irrevocably committed to countering the influence of the Holy Ghost.

Satan will always be thwarted. He may win some battles, but he will never win the war. He will have the power to bruise our heels, but we have the power to crush his head. He lost in the Sacred Grove during Joseph Smith's First Vision when, "just at this moment of great alarm, I [Joseph Smith] saw a pillar of light exactly over my head, above the brightness of the sun, which descended gradually until it fell upon me. It no sooner appeared than I found myself delivered from the enemy which held me bound" (Joseph Smith History 16-17). Joseph Smith then proceeded to move forward with the restoration of the gospel of Jesus Christ in these latter days.

Satan lost in his battle with Alma the younger, who shortly after being struck dumb for three days testified that "after wading through much tribulation, repenting nigh unto death, the Lord in mercy hath seen fit to snatch me out of an everlasting burning...My soul hath been redeemed from the gall of bitterness and bonds of iniquity. I was in the darkest abyss; but now I behold the marvelous light of God" (Book of Mormon, Mosiah 27:28-29). Alma became one of the greatest prophets in the Book of Mormon and devoted his life to bringing others to repentance and teaching them the saving ordinances of the gospel.

And the prince of lies certainly lost in the Garden of Eden after Eve partook of the fruit of knowledge of good and evil. Lucifer wanted to force us to be obedient. He wanted to take our agency away and he wanted the glory all to himself but in the end, it was because of him and his temptation to partake of the fruit, that we have our agency and the ability to return to our Father in Heaven. In the story of Moses, Pharaoh and his people suffered greatly until he agreed to let the children of Israel free. But even then, Satan still held onto Pharaoh's heart, and he sent his army after Moses and those he rescued. Satan lost after Moses parted the Red Sea and all of Pharaoh's people were swallowed up and drowned. It was shortly thereafter that Moses received the Ten Commandments.

Although my personal story cannot be compared to Joseph Smith's, or Alma's, or Adam and Eve's or Moses', my experience with overcoming the adversary at a very low point in my life was just as real. We've all been there. We've all experienced the darkest of days when moving forward seemed like an impossible task. But what each of us needs to decide is whether we are going to stay and fight or are we going to allow the adversary to win. Because it is a choice.

'Let Us All Press On' has always been one of my favorite hymns, but after my experience, it became even more precious to me. Let us remember to press on in the face of our battles, because winning against evil should be our only option.

Let us all press on in the work of the Lord,
That when life is o'er we may gain a reward;
In the fight for right let us wield a sword,
The mighty sword of truth.
We will not retreat, though our numbers may be few
When compared with the opposite host in view;
But an unseen power will aid me and you
In the glorious cause of truth.
If we do what's right we have no need to fear,
For the Lord, our helper, will ever be near;
In the days of trial his Saints he will cheer,
And prosper the cause of truth.
Fear not, though the enemy deride;
Courage, for the Lord is on our side.

We will heed not what the wicked may say,

But the Lord alone we will obey.

Evan Stephens, The Church of Jesus Christ of Latter-Day Saints
Hymnal # 243

Chapter 9

Falling Through the Stairs

The moment I realized that writing this book was a journey I would inevitably take, I became almost paralyzed with fear, and my head began swimming with doubts. What if no one read it? What if people read it and then hated it? What if my words didn't make sense, or I struggled to tie my dreams together with gospel principles? How would I react when others criticized this task given to me by God? Would they understand that it was truly a labor of love? So much anxiety; so little faith.

I was clearly no expert on spiritual gifts, so my first thought was to ask friends and family for help. I sent out several emails and text messages, explaining the concept of the book and then asked what their spiritual gift was and how God used it to answer their prayers. I was surprised, and frustrated, when only a few individuals responded. Not a great start. I reached out to a few more people, and received the empty sound of crickets as my only response. After my second attempt had failed miserably, I was grumbling to myself, feeling defeated that I couldn't get any help on what felt like a monumental burden. I was standing at my kitchen sink, angrily washing dishes when Heavenly Father lovingly reminded me of whom I should be seeking guidance from. Very clearly, and very loudly, He said, "Stop asking others, and start seeking help from the One that has put you on this path." Oops. A little spiritual shove in the right direction never hurt anyone, right?

I immediately stopped doing the dishes, grabbed a pen and paper and sat down. I said a prayer of gratitude, invited the spirit, and pled for inspiration as I began a very basic outline. I pondered all the dreams and visions I'd had over the years and jotted down what spiritual lessons I learned from each one. I thought about how other gifts could be used to teach those same lessons and what that would look like. I remembered stories from scriptures, prophets, and church conferences that would also be applicable. As the thoughts continued to flow, peace began taking over where once there was fear and anxiety. I simply needed to have enough faith to take that first step with Heavenly Father's help and walk down the path He had clearly placed before me. It was at this point that I was quietly reminded of Rebekah.

In the book of Genesis, we learn of Rebekah, who was going about her daily chores of collecting water at the community well, when a stranger came asking for a drink. She did not ask who he was or where he came from, and she didn't grumble about having to stop her chores to serve her fellow man. Rebekah simply responded in kind by serving him and attending to his needs and fetching water for all his camels. In fact, "she hastened" to give her pitcher of water to the man, and she hastened to give drink to the camels. The stranger was so enamored by this beautiful and kind young woman that he asked if there was room enough for him to lodge with her family in their home. There was, and she invited him to meet her brother. (Old Testament, Genesis 24:18-23)

The stranger introduced himself to Rebekah's brother, Laban, as the servant of Abraham, who had sent him on the journey to find a wife for his son, Isaac. The servant requested Rebekah's hand in marriage on behalf of Abraham, and Laban agreed but requested that Rebekah stay at least ten additional days with her family before they departed. The servant, in a rush to get back home to his master, requested that they leave immediately. Laban called Rebekah and asked if she would agree to leave. (Genesis 24:51-57) "And [Rebekah] said, I will go." (Genesis 24:58) Again, she didn't ask questions, she didn't seek the guidance of others, she simply said I will go. A short three-word phrase that we would all do well to remember when confronted with the unknown paths before us.

While I sat there reviewing my outline, thinking about this amazing woman of the Old Testament, I strongly felt encouraged to make sure the book was ten chapters long, which seemed silly at the time. I wasn't quite sure why I felt so strongly about it, and simply based it on my slightly obsessive tendencies to have good even numbers. Ten chapters was perfect. What I realized shortly thereafter was that I only had nine chapters listed in my outline. I was one chapter short, but I knew there was plenty of time to figure the rest out later. Regardless, I was determined to go and do, just as Rebekah had done.

Days turned into weeks and weeks turned into months. I had writer's block a few times that lasted longer than I hoped, but more often than not, I was given inspiration at the exact moment I needed it. I was so close to being done but was still plagued with only having nine chapters. At one point, I simply decided that nine was enough, but then God lovingly reminded me once again that I needed to seek his help. Would I ever learn? Was I ever going to say, 'I will go', and trust in His plan? Would I ever fully embrace the Old Testament book Proverbs 3:5-6 which is a stark reminder to do just that. We are admonished to, "Trust in the Lord with all thine heart; and lean not unto thine own understanding. In all thy ways acknowledge him, and he shall direct thy paths." Apparently, I still needed more practice.

I kept going back over all my dreams, but nothing felt right. It was during this time that my husband and I were exhausting ourselves with trying to find a home to buy. We had sold our house and had been renting a small condominium until something else came along. Six months, and seven failed home offers later, and both of us felt like giving up. We wanted to stay in the area for multiple reasons, but every time we tried to make that happen, the proverbial door was slammed in our face.

The previous year, I was surfing on the internet, looking at old farmhouses (a favorite mind-numbing pastime for me), when I stumbled on one that was for sale. I remember thinking that that beautiful home, with so much history and character, would not last long on the market, and the individual who purchased it would be very lucky indeed. Several months went by and as I frustratingly looked once again for a home, that farmhouse popped back up and was still listed for sale. I was shocked. And the price was much lower than it had been before. Several thoughts ran through my mind all at once. How was this gorgeous one hundred-and fifty-year-old home still available? And at that price? Could no one see the elegance under the old? Wasn't there someone out there that would love the house enough to restore her to her original beauty? Would my husband be interested in going to look at it? But it was four hours away. But it was closer to our son and his family. But we'd have to move away from the church family we had grown to love. But the house had so much potential. But it's not what we were looking for. But we've been going around in circles trying to find something here. But. But. But.

The next day I nonchalantly brought up the old farmhouse to my husband. As I expected, he wasn't very excited about the idea because of the amount of time, money and work it would take just to make the house livable, so I let it go. After church the following Sunday, he suggested that we reach out to the realtor and get some additional information. He was following the prompting to go and do. The following afternoon, I spoke with the selling agent and quickly realized that I would need a lot of help in convincing my husband to buy this house. It wasn't falling down per se, but it would need a lot more love and attention, and money, than we had originally anticipated.

We spent the next few days going over all the work it would need and the amount of time it would take us. We did research on the cost of several big-ticket items and reached out to friends that we knew in the construction industry for their advice. After we did as much research as possible, based on the limited amount of information that we had, we scheduled a showing and took that four-hour drive. Purchasing this home was not looking favorable, and I began to understand why it was still on the market, but regardless of how pessimistic both of us were, we followed through on the prompting that we had received. We were going, and we were doing. It was during our drive down that the strangest little prick of a dream tickled the back of my mind. I mentally rolled my eyes and pushed the memory of that dream aside because it was silly and nonsensical and was not spiritual in any way.

We will all have moments of doubt and uncertainty in our lives. Moments that seem to not make sense. Times when only a miracle would need to occur for things to work out. Promptings that cause us to scratch our head in disbelief. Or a promised blessing that makes you laugh at the absurdity of it, like our sweet Sarah in the Old Testament, who would end up being Rebekah's mother-in-law. Loving, faithful Sarah.

Sarah was married to Abraham for several years and, through the covenant, God promised them that He would, "make of thee a great nation, and will bless thee above measure and thou shalt be a blessing unto thy seed after thee" (Abraham 2:9). Abraham and Sarah were promised an entire nation and yet, Sarah suffered with infertility. As was the law back then, if a wife could not conceive a child, she was required to provide her husband with another woman to marry, however the first wife would always maintain authority over any additional women that were brought into the family. In Sarah's case, she gave her maid Hagar to Abraham to wed, and they immediately began having children while Sarah was still baren. Sarah's only prayer was to have a child, and even though she clung to the promise that she would have seed, her hope of becoming a mother dwindled as the years went by.

At the ripe young age of 99, Abraham was entertaining three holy men that had arrived in his community. Sarah, who was now 89 years of age, was going about her duties as wife by making bread for their unexpected visitors. While in her tent, she happened to overhear the conversation between her husband and her guests. "And they said unto [Abraham], Where is Sarah thy wife? And he said, Behold, in the tent. And he said, I will certainly return unto thee according to the time of life; and, lo, Sarah thy wife shall have a son. And Sarah heard it in the tent door" (Genesis 18:9-10).

"Therefore Sarah laughed within herself" (Genesis 18:12).

I'm not sure any of us would have reacted differently than Sarah. We would all find it humorous if we were told we'd have a child at the age of 89. How truly absurd. And yet, "Is anything too hard for the Lord" (Old Testament, Genesis 18:14)? James E Faust gave us a wonderful reminder of the possibility of miracles when he said, "The Lord can do remarkable miracles with a person of ordinary ability who is humble, faithful, and diligent in serving the Lord and seeks to improve himself" (Acting For Ourselves and Not Being Acted Upon; General Conference, October 1995). We would certainly need a miracle to occur in order for us to buy that dilapidated building and make it our next home.

We pulled up to the house, and that tickle of a dream came back again, and again I dismissed it as ridiculous. As we got out of the car and took our first look at the house, my initial thought was that I hoped the roof didn't collapse on top of us. My second thought was to question how the house not had been condemned yet. We walked around back, gingerly took the rotted stairs to the back door, and hesitantly entered at our own risk. The musty smell that immediately hit me was almost overwhelming. The wallpaper was peeling, the floors were creaky, and the dust seemed to be three inches thick. I walked down the short hallway to the front door, turned around, and froze. Unlike Sarah who laughed to herself, I was unquestionably more uncouth and less ladylike. I snorted and then guffawed. I didn't need to see any more of that sketchy, ramshackle farmhouse. I knew, without a doubt, that it was meant to be ours. A miracle indeed. Heavenly Father really does have a sense of humor.

The images of that dream from many years previous came flooding back in an instant. My husband and I were diving through hundreds of miles of wheat fields when we came upon an old, abandoned house sitting

92

in the middle of nowhere. We both got out and went up to the front porch to peek through the window when I realized that the door was open. As we walked inside, I noticed a room to the left and a room to the right with a grand staircase in the foyer. My husband was meandering throughout the house when I decided to venture up the stairs. I got about halfway up when a few of the steps splintered and broke. I screamed as I fell through steps up to my waist. I tried to pull myself out of the hole to no avail, but thankfully my husband came around the corner and proceeded to rescue me from my stuck position. The following morning, I woke up and told him about my crazy night, and we both laughed it off as one of those random dreams we all get.

As I stood looking at the rooms to the right and to the left with that imposing staircase in front of me, I knew I had been here before. That silly, non-sensical dream that meant nothing, not only became a reality, but I could easily imagine Heavenly Father looking down with a smile saying, "Here's your tenth chapter."

Miracles. In today's modern world, Google defines miracles as an extraordinary event in the physical world that surpasses all known human or natural powers and is ascribed to a supernatural cause. Whereas the church defines miracles as an extraordinary event caused by the power of God. When we talk about miracles, our first thoughts are of those beautiful stories in the scriptures that tell of what Jesus did during His ministry: turning the water into wine, feeding the five thousand, healing the sick, restoring sight to the blind, raising the dead, and of course, His resurrection. We may also think about other stories like Moses when he parted the Red Sea, the donkey that spoke to his rider, the manna that fell from heaven. Or Book of Mormon stories such as the earthquake that crumbled the prison walls while Alma and Amulek were being held prisoner, allowing them to walk free while the guards were buried. Or when the Brother of Jared saw the finger of God when He touched the sixteen stones, or Joseph Smith in the Sacred Grove.

The scriptures are filled with miracles of times past, but do we see those types of extraordinary events in our own lives? We are often reminded that faith precedes the miracle, and if we have faith as the grain of a mustard seed, we could move mountains. But has anyone ever tried to actually move a mountain? We are cautioned about the need for faith in the Book of Mormon in Ether 12:18 which states that "neither at any time hath any wrought miracles until after their faith." Miracles will not always present themselves in the form of grand events, but rather in the small and simple experiences of ordinary people in everyday life.

It was a miracle that we were not able to find a home to purchase in the area we wanted to live. It was a miracle that God urged my husband to drive four hours to look at a house that needed more work than either of us wanted to tackle. It was a miracle that our old farmhouse had not already been purchased. And then there's the miracle of my gift. My dream was the answer to a prayer that had not even been uttered, let alone thought of. My dream that was years in the making. My dream that allowed me to see a miracle unfold before my eyes.

Each of us is given the opportunity to see miracles in our lives every day but let us not forget that our spiritual gifts and talents are miracles as well. If your gift is that of not passing judgement, then you may see a miracle in the face of a lost soul who simply needs a friend to offer an encouraging word, a healing touch, or a loving smile. And your ability to love that lost soul without judgement will allow you to see the miracle of the atonement work as you walk beside your friend on their journey back to God's kingdom. If your gift is believing the testimony of others, then you will certainly see a miracle in the innocence of a child who bravely shares their simple belief that God loves them. And if you are blessed with the humble gift of asking for help, whether for yourself or for others, then you will surely be given the opportunity to see miracles unfold in the lives of those who choose to serve, especially when it's hard or inconvenient.

94

Miracles remind us that anything is possible and that we are constantly being supported by a loving Heavenly Father who knows our very soul. In 1830, the Lord revealed this very important doctrine to Joseph Smith when He said, "For I am God, and mine arm is not shortened; and I will show miracles, signs and wonders unto all those who believe on my name." It takes faith to believe miracles will happen. It takes faith to wait for them to unfold. It takes faith to see them for what they are. Faith truly does precede the miracle.

May each of us strive to use our gifts to be a little more like Rebekah and say, "I will go". As we act on those promptings to go, may we also use our gifts to aspire to be a little more like Sarah and recognize those miracles as God's promises being fulfilled. And may we never forget the little things, the everyday miracles in our lives, as described by Walt Whitman in his beautiful work titled 'Miracles'.

Why, who makes much of a miracle?
As to me I know of nothing else but miracles,
Whether I walk the streets of Manhattan,
Or dart my sight over the roofs of houses toward the sky,
Or wade with naked feet along the beach just in the edge of the water,
Or stand under trees in the woods,
Or talk by day with any one I love, or sleep in the bed at night with any one I love,
Or sit at table at dinner with the rest,
Or look at strangers opposite me riding in the car,
Or watch honey-bees busy around the hive of a summer forenoon,
Or animals feeding in the fields,
Or birds, or the wonderfulness of insects in the air,
Or the wonderfulness of the sundown, or of stars shining so quiet and bright,

Or the exquisite delicate thin curve of the new moon in spring;
These with the rest, one and all, are to me miracles,
The whole referring, yet each distinct and in its place.
To me every hour of the light and dark is a miracle,
Every cubic inch of space is a miracle,
Every square yard of the surface of the earth is spread with the same,
Every foot of the interior swarms with the same.
To me the sea is a continual miracle,
The fishes that swim—the rocks—the motion of the waves—the ships with men in them,
What stranger miracles are there?

"Miracles," Whitman's Leaves of Grass, 1856, Fowler and Wells

Chapter 10

Determine, Understand, Utilize

My favorite Disney movie has always been "The Little Mermaid". I am a sucker for the classic animated movies with cute love stories and happy endings. Beyond that, I've always had a deep love and appreciation for the water. In fact, I'm pretty sure that I was a mermaid in a previous life. But my love for this particular movie goes beyond the basic storyline. From the moment I first heard Ariel's flawless voice, provided by the real-life Jody Benson, sing "Part of Your World," I was mesmerized. The tone of her voice, the control, the innocence she portrayed, and the longing to be a part of something more simply grabbed my attention. Through a series of events, Ariel meets and quickly falls for a charming young prince named Eric. But Ariel is a mermaid, and Eric is a human. Undaunted, in Ariel's quest for wanting to be a part of the human world, she falls prey to the cunningness of Ursula the sea witch, who proposes a deal with her. Ursula agrees to give Ariel legs and make her human in exchange for Ariel's gift of singing. Reluctantly, Ariel agrees, and Ursula takes her voice as she transforms from mermaid tail to human legs. And Ursula's evil plan to take over the ocean is set in motion. Thankfully, good triumphed over evil in the end. Ariel was given her voice back, she married her beau, and they lived happily ever after.

I have severe vocal envy, and as a result I have often compared myself to Ariel - I am convinced that my singing voice was stolen somewhere between the pre-existence and mortality. Either that or Heavenly Father is keeping my beautiful vocals safe, with the promise that I can have them back if I work really hard and return to Him when this life is finished. I say that light heartedly, but my singing voice is no laughing matter. God was generous in providing me with spiritual gifts, but singing is not one of them. I love to sing, and I've taken many lessons with a number of highly gifted vocal coaches but singing beautifully is simply not a talent I will possess in this lifetime.

I struggled for many years trying to understand precisely what my talents were, and like many individuals, felt I didn't really have any. Yes, I have my revelatory dreams and visions, but those are gifts that God gives me when I need them. They are not talents that I can practice and get better at.

Throughout my journey of finding out what my talents are, I did what I felt were all the right things: I applied the primary answers of praying, pondering, and studying. I read my Patriarchal Blessing (an inspired prayer given to worthy members of the church, which contains personal guidance, comfort, and direction from the Lord) many times. I researched talks and articles on talents, I tried my hand at many different activities, and sought the advice of family, friends, and church members. It wasn't until years later, while meeting with my Stake President on a completely different matter, that my answers began to unfold. At some point during our discussion, the conversation turned to our mutual love of reading. He suggested that I read a book called "Achieving Your Life Mission" by Randal A. Wright. He then asked if he could give me a Priesthood blessing. Of course I agreed and I will never forget the sweetest words that were said. I was reminded that Heavenly Father loved me and that I needed to continue seeking out my gifts. I immediately went home and purchased that very book. It was during this time that I was guided on a path that has helped me learn to recognize and understand my gifts and lead me to have a deeper understanding and appreciation for those I do have.

One of my favorite stories in the Old Testament is that of Abigail, a lesser-known heroine, whose gifts brought about much good, though I'm sure it was not in the way she expected. According to "Legends of the Jews', written by L. Ginzberg, Abigail was considered to be one of the most beautiful women in history, but her gift of beauty did not correlate to her being blessed with a good and righteous husband. In fact, her situation was quite the opposite. Abigail was married to Nabal, a man described as being "churlish and evil in his doings" (1 Samuel 25:3). Nabal took advantage of his station and as a result, created many enemies, and made Abigail's life rather difficult. One of his adversaries was David, who had previously defeated Goliath with a sling. Nabal's selfish and deceitful choices enraged David who, in turn, sought to take the life of Nabal. Thankfully, Abigail intercepted David as he journeyed to carry out his wrath on Nabal and his people. Her gift of diplomacy and courage, and her calming demeanor in the face of a powerful and agitated David, kept David from seeking vengeance upon Nabal, which would have derailed the plans God had in store for the future king (1 Samuel 25:4-35). Abigail's gifts were not fully employed while under the thumb of Nabal. It wasn't until God needed her prophetic words to deliver David from his path of retribution that Abigail was blessed to partake in the gifts that God had given her.

Another beautiful example of one whose gifts felt late in coming is that of Moroni in the Book of Mormon in Ether Chapter 12. The Lord commanded Moroni to record many miracles brought about by faith, however Moroni expressed his anxiety to the Lord because of his inability to write when he said:

> Lord, the Gentiles will mock at these things, because of our weakness in writing; for Lord thou has made us mighty in word by faith, but thou has not made us mighty in writing And thou has made us that we could write but little, because of the awkwardness of our hands Thou hast also made our words powerful and great, even that we cannot write them; wherefore, when we write we behold our weakness, and stumble because of the placing of our words (Ether 12:23-25).

99

Moroni received a humbling response when God answered his plea with the following words in verse 27 which states, "And if men come unto me I will show unto them their weakness. I give unto men weakness that they may be humble; and my grace is sufficient for all men that humble themselves before me; for if they humble themselves before me, and have faith in me, then will I make weak things become strong unto them." Moroni did not have the gift of writing, but he did have the gift of faith that ultimately led to what would become the Book of Mormon.

A well-known story that illustrates the importance of differing talents is that of Martha and Mary in Luke chapter 10 in the New Testament. Jesus "entered into a certain village: and a certain woman named Martha received him unto her house." (Luke 10:38) Martha's Christlike talent of serving others was clearly on display when she was "cumbered about much serving" while Jesus was teaching those around Him. But Martha, not understanding there are many ways to show love to others, complained that her sister Mary was not helping serve but instead was sitting at Jesus' feet to hear His words. Mary was embracing her talent of listening and learning by doing just that, and not being influenced by others' opinions of her. Jesus lovingly replied to Martha's complaint by responding with, "Mary hath chosen the good part, which shall not be taken away from her." (Luke 10:39-42) Both of these women loved the Lord. Both women wanted to serve Him. Both women did so in their own unique way by using their individual talents.

If you are like me and have struggled to understand or recognize your own talents, please do not give up. Our talents come in many forms. Some are physical, some are spiritual, and some are emotional. In my journey of finding out what is unique to me, I thought about what I loved to do in my spare time (sports, hiking, reading), what I was good at in high school (math and English), and the many things that brought excitement and peace to my life (my children and grandchildren). During this process,

I realized that I didn't always acknowledge, appreciate, and utilize my talents the way I should have.

I excelled in English in all levels of my education and could have made that one of my focuses in college, but that is not what I wanted to do with my life. Even now, I thoroughly enjoy reading in my downtime. And I find creative writing to be fulfilling and edifying. But what is one thing that the church encourages us to do as a matter of genealogy and as a gift to our posterity? Journaling. Recently our Relief Society lesson was on this very subject and I sat there inwardly cringing. As much as writing in general brings me joy, and as many times as I've tried to follow this council, I have failed at it. Every time. Because I cannot find a way to love it or be motivated by it. One of my talents is writing and I do not enjoy journaling. I know it sounds crazy but, sadly, it's true. In my distaste for it, I didn't feel as though journaling was so important until reality hit me when I read a quote by President Joseph F. Smith which states, "Every son and every daughter of God has received some talent, and each will be held to strict account for the use or misuse to which it is put" ("Gospel Principles"; Chpt 34, "Developing Our Talents"). Oof .

When we give the perfect gift to those we love, we want the recipient to appreciate the time and thought and effort we took to select that gift. We want them to feel how important they are to us. And when that gift is set aside and not used, or even worse, thrown away or donated to charity, our hearts can feel broken. The same applies to our gifts from God. He gives them to us to bless our lives and help us endure our trials; He gives them to us so we can serve others; He gives them to us to help us in our battle against the adversary; He gives them to us because he wants us to know how important we are to Him. When we do not use our gifts, or we discard them like empty Chinese food takeout containers destined for the wasteland, we are forsaking a sacred blessing given by the very hand of our Creator.

In contrast to not knowing or understanding our gifts and talents, perhaps you can think of someone who seems to have more gifts than any one person should, someone who is annoyingly talented? Two individuals come to mind for me, and they both give me envy anxiety, which I say with the utmost love. My brother-in-law was one such person. He was irritatingly good at everything he did. He was a chef, an author, raced motorcycles, wrote music, played a mean bass guitar, knew the scriptures inside and out, and loved to read Isaiah (who does that?). In addition to this list of individually monumental gifts, he was a particularly phenomenal artist, which allowed him to have an extraordinary career in custom design jewelry. I also have a friend whose talents and gifts are so numerous that it almost defies logic. She can draw, paint, sing, play instruments, and make Montessori toys. She writes children's books, sews, gardens, and carves wood. She's also working at rebuilding a dune buggy - fiberglass body, engine and all. She has the gift of teaching and the gift of learning, and her love and faith in the Lord is exceptional. Several years ago, I asked her how she was able to do so many things and do them so well. Her answer was not what I was expecting. She chuckled and said, "I'm too dumb to realize I can't do it." She then followed it up with, "I do honestly believe, though, that it all comes down to trying - that's how I found out I'm terrible at Physics!", demonstrating her gift of honesty and her ability to make others laugh. Her answer made me realize that, like my brother-in-law, we each truly do have the power, with God's help, to accomplish any task, exceed any goal, and achieve any dream that we set our mind and heart to.

Each of us has been blessed with unique gifts and talents, and just like fingerprints, no two are the same. Where we lack in one, God makes up for it elsewhere. I may never be talented enough to express my love for the Savior by singing a solo during church services, but I can add my voice to that of the congregation in an effort to invite the spirit into my heart. I will never have the gift of healing others physically, but I have the gift of knowing that I can be healed through faith and Priesthood blessings.

So where do you start in your journey of determining, understanding, and utilizing your sacred gifts? It should not be a surprise when I say that you need to start with the same Primary answers that I started with. Sincerely pray to your Heavenly Father for discernment in recognizing your gifts. Study the many different types of gifts in the scriptures. Ask for guidance through the power of a Priesthood blessing. Read and study your Patriarchal Blessing and write down each gift and talent mentioned there. Read or listen to conference talks specific to talents and gifts. Ask family and close friends what talents they see in you. Make a list of subjects you excelled in at school, different types of skills you do well, and any spiritual qualities that come naturally to you. And then pray again. And again. And again, until you begin to have the understanding that you seek. We are taught in 1Timothy 4:14-16 to "Neglect not the gift that is in [you]Meditate upon these things; give thyself wholly to them; that thy profiting may appear to all."

Once you begin to recognize your gifts and talents, you will need to put them into practice. In doing so, remember that you will not be perfect in the beginning. Each of our talents and gifts requires practice, patience, self-discipline, and more than a little humility as we refine and work to improve our sacred blessings. Do not try to run before you can walk. We are constantly reminded that we learn line upon line, precept upon precept, even when it comes to our talents. If you stumble, and I promise you will, remember the encouragement that Elder Dieter F. Uchtdorf gave us when he said:

Sometimes we feel discouraged because we are not 'more' of something – more spiritual, respected, intelligent, healthy, rich, friendly, or capable. We don't need to be 'more' of anything to start to become the person God intended us to become. God will take you as you are at this very moment and begin to work with you. All you need is a willing heart, a desire to believe, and trust in the Lord. (General Conference, October 2015 – "It Works Wonderfully!")

And let me remind you that I didn't realize my ability to write was a talent until God plopped the task of writing this book in my lap, a few years after I became a grandmother. So please don't feel discouraged if it takes you a while to get there. The important thing is that you intentionally begin to seek after these things.

One of the most important things to remember is that you are not starting from scratch when it comes to your talents. As premortal beings, we brought with us the talents that we acquired in the pre-existence. Elder Bruce R. McConkie stated it best when he said:

All the spirits of men (and women), while yet in the Eternal Presence, developed aptitudes, talents, capacities, and abilities of every sort, kind, and degree. During the long expanse of life which then was, an infinite variety of talents and abilities came into being. As the ages rolled, no two spirits remained alike. Mozart became a musician; Einstein centered his interest in mathematics; Michelangelo turned his attention to painting. Abraham and Moses and all of the prophets sought and obtained the talent for spirituality. When we pass from preexistence to mortality, we bring with us the traits and talents there developed. True, we forget what went before because we are here being tested, but the capacities and abilities that then were ours are yet resident within us. Mozart is still a musician; Einstein retains his mathematical abilities; Michelangelo his artistic talent; Abraham, Moses, and the prophets their spiritual talents and abilities. And all men with their infinitely varied talents and personalities pick up the course of progression where they left it off when they left the heavenly realms. (The Mortal Messiah, 4 vols. [1979–81], 1:23, 25)

It is my prayer that each of us has the desire to learn of and hone every gift and talent that God has given us. Utilize them now so we can perfect them in the eternities. May we strive to honor those gifts by using them to better ourselves, to serve those in need, and most importantly, to glorify the One who bestowed them upon each of us. Just as we can expect to stand before our Maker to be judged for our deeds, so will we be held accountable for the use or misuse of our gifts and talents. A sobering reminder of this was given to us by Elder Marvin J. Ashton when he stated:

One of the great tragedies of life, it seems to me, is when a person classifies himself as someone who has no talents or gifts. When, in disgust or discouragement, we allow ourselves to reach depressive levels of despair because of our demeaning self-appraisal, it is a sad day for us and a sad day in the eyes of God. For us to conclude that we have no gifts when we judge ourselves by stature, intelligence, grade-point average, wealth, power, position, or external appearance is not only unfair but unreasonable. God has given each of us one or more special talents. It is up to each of us to search for and build upon the gifts which God has given. (Conference Report, Oct. 1987, 23; or Ensign, Nov. 1987, 20)

Our gifts and talents were given for eternal purposes. We cannot choose what we are innately good at, but we can always choose how hard we try to make the best of what we have been given. As in the parable of the talents, I desperately want to hear my Savior say, "Well done, thou good and faithful servant: thou hast been faithful over a few things, I will make thee ruler over many things: enter thou into the joy of thy lord" (Matthew 25:21).

May we not let our securities, or our insecurities, get in the way of discovering the many spiritual, physical and emotional gifts that God has given us, and may we all be too dumb to realize that we can't do what our heart desires. I may even try singing again.

I URGE YOU,

WITH ALL THE HOPE OF MY HEART,

TO PRAY TO UNDERSTAND YOUR SPIRITUAL GIFTS.

TO *CULTIVATE,*

USE,

AND *EXPAND* THEM,

EVEN MORE THAN YOU EVER HAVE.

YOU WILL *CHANGE THE WORLD* AS YOU DO SO.

President Russell M. Nelson,
General Conference, October 2018 - "Sisters' Participation in the Gathering of Israel"

I have included the gifts and talents that I've seen in my life and in the lives of others. And writing this book has motivated me to be better at owning my spiritual journey of determining, understanding, and utilizing more of the gifts that God has given me. It is my hope and prayer that as you begin, or continue your own journey, that God touches your heart as He did mine. Please use the following journal pages to help you discover the gifts that have been sprinkled upon you like fairy dust from the open windows of Heaven. And once you figure them out, may you own them and love them like the gifts they truly are.

Spiritual Gifts

Has a belief in Jesus Christ ♦ Follows the council of the Prophet ♦ Resiliency during trials ♦ Non-judgmental ♦ Leadership ♦ Expresses gratitude ♦ Pays tithing ♦ Studies scriptures ♦ Shares testimony ♦ Fasts with intention ♦ Leads by a good example ♦ Waits on God's timing ♦ Has faith to be healed ♦ Follows the Word of Wisdom ♦ Keeps an eternal perspective ♦ Keeps sacred things sacred ♦ Accepts and fulfills callings ♦ Obeys the commandments ♦ Offers Prayer ♦ Has the Spirit of Discernment ♦ Understands scriptures ♦ Has charity ♦ Shows mercy ♦ Teaches with the spirit ♦ Easily relies on faith ♦ Beholds angels and spirits ♦ Wisdom/Knowledge ♦ Recognizes small miracles ♦ Spirit of Revelation ♦ Member missionary ♦ Obedience ♦ Ministers to others ♦ Dreams and Visions ♦ Listens to the promptings of the Spirit ♦ Honors covenants ♦ Recognizes blessings ♦ Sees others as sons and daughters of God ♦

Physical Gifts

Gardening ♦ Food storage ♦ Public speaking ♦ Painting ♦ Technology ♦ Interior design ♦ Sewing ♦ Photography ♦ Woodworking ♦ Singing ♦ Self-defense ♦ Money management ♦ Playing a musical instrument ♦ Teaching ♦ Mechanics ♦ Writing (music, poetry, books) ♦ Healing others ♦ Fitness ♦ Cooking/Baking ♦ Serving others ♦ Sports ♦ DIY projects ♦ Fashion ♦ Dancing ♦ Acting ♦ Computers ♦ Homemaking ♦ Organizational skills ♦ Speaking a foreign language ♦ Has a house of order ♦ Endurance ♦ Networking ♦ Patriotism ♦ Trade skills ♦ Team building ♦ Health and wellness ♦ Science/Math/English ♦

Emotional Gifts

Has a sense of humor ♦ Self-Confident ♦ Respects others' opinions ♦ Weeps with others ♦ Honesty ♦ Asks for help ♦ Avoids contention ♦ Has and shows empathy ♦ Does not hold grudges ♦ Quick to apologize ♦ Shows gratitude freely and often ♦ Has courage over fears ♦ Listens to others ♦ Makes friends easily ♦ Patient ♦ Accepts personal responsibility ♦ Sees the best in others ♦ Learns quickly and/or easily ♦ Self-motivating ♦ Motivates others ♦ Gives grace ♦ Controls anger and/or frustration ♦ Shows kindness ♦ Gentleness ♦ Gives encouragement ♦ Loves others easily ♦ Affectionate ♦ Forgives quickly ♦ Communicates well ♦ Supports others in their trials ♦ Empathetic/Sympathetic ♦ Optimistic ♦ Able to problem-solve ♦ Conflict resolution ♦ Self-awareness ♦ Logical ♦ Keeps an eternal perceptive ♦ A peacemaker ♦ Always happy ♦ Gives freely of time and talents ♦

1. My gifts are:

_____

_____

_____

_____

_____

_____

_____

_____

_____

_____

_____

_____

_____

2. Classes I excelled in at school:

_____

_____

_____

_____

_____

_____

_____

_____

_____

_____

_____

_____

_____

3. Emotions/feelings that come easily to me:

_____

_____

_____

_____

_____

_____

_____

_____

_____

_____

_____

_____

_____

_____

_____

4. Activities that I enjoy doing in my spare time:

_____

_____

_____

_____

_____

_____

_____

_____

_____

_____

_____

_____

_____

_____

5. Gifts and talents mentioned in my Patriarchal Blessing:

_____

_____

_____

_____

_____

_____

_____

_____

_____

_____

_____

_____

_____

_____

6. Things that others have said I'm good at:

_____

_____

_____

_____

_____

_____

_____

_____

_____

_____

_____

_____

_____

7. Ways I've been able to bless the lives of others:

_____

_____

_____

_____

_____

_____

_____

_____

_____

_____

_____

_____

_____

_____

8. Ways I can use my gifts as a weapon against the adversary:

_____

_____

_____

_____

_____

_____

_____

_____

_____

_____

_____

_____

_____

9. God has used my gift/talent to bless my life by:

_____

_____

_____

_____

_____

_____

_____

_____

_____

_____

_____

_____

_____

_____

10. *Things I can do to strengthen my gift:*

_____

_____

_____

_____

_____

_____

_____

_____

_____

_____

_____

_____

_____

WE SHOULD SEEK AFTER SPIRITUAL GIFTS.

THEY CAN LEAD US TO GOD.

THEY CAN SHIELD US FROM THE POWER OF THE ADVERSARY.

THEY CAN COMPENSATE FOR OUR INADEQUACIES AND REPAIR OUR IMPERFECTIONS.

Dallin H. Oaks, "Spiritual Gifts," Ensign, September 1986